I0464251

Dedicated to B

You are missed

ISBN #: 978-1-304-54420-9

By Joseph Alexander

Retail Relationships

Unleash the power of customer intimacy to increase sales and

Connect with your customers

Table of Contents

Introduction

Introduction

When speaking with groups of retailers and retail salespeople, I routinely kick things off by asking those in attendance to raise their hands if, back when they were kids, they dreamed of a life in retail and retail sales. Not surprisingly, there are very few people, if any, who raise their hands. It is a great way to break the ice and loosen up the group, and guaranteed to get a hearty chuckle. It is also an entertaining method of addressing the elephant in the room, as this may not be exactly where anyone expected their professional life to be at that moment. A career in retail is not one of the glamour careers you brag about to your friends and family. There is no Doctorate of Retail Sales. Most of us who have found ourselves in retail arrived here out of necessity; we needed the paycheck.

A good friend of mine, who is a veterinarian, once told me that she got into Veterinary Medicine because she hated sales. Guess what? She was dismayed to find that after 9 years of schooling that she *was* in sales. That's right, the Vet Clinic sells services and products too.

In fact, when you think about it, almost every profession involves some level of selling, and at one time or another, we have all sold something. Even the dating ritual involves selling yourself. A mantra I try to instill in retailers and business owners is, "Nothing happens until somebody sells something!" There is nothing to service, advertise or manufacture if first somebody does not sell something.

Sales is not only an admirable profession, but YOU make the wheels of this world go around. If you sell for a living, you are responsible for the paychecks of everyone in your company! YOU are the straw that stirs the drink. YOU make things happen. And with that in mind, it is imperative that you are not only well-trained but that you maintain a well-organized and well-planned, ongoing training.

"Nothing happens until somebody

sells something!"

It's time to hold your head up high, take pride in working retail, and strive to be the best you can be. When talking with salespeople, I am struck by an interesting discovery: I find that most salespeople are unaware of the importance of their job. Not only are they responsible for generating income for their company, they are also the face of the company. When you walk into Home Depot, you don't meet with the CEO, you meet with Melissa, the 19-year-old mother-of-one who works part-time and goes to school part-time. And if you have a great customer experience, it's because of Melissa.

One afternoon I was working as a sales manager at a furniture store when I greeted a woman and her middle-aged daughter in my usual warm, engaging style. Both were very cordial and friendly, and after the greeting I quickly discovered what they seeking that day and set out to give them some ideas of what we had to solve their issue. As we made our way around the store the older woman stopped at a display of bedroom furniture and inexplicably broke down sobbing. I was blindsided by her emotional display but moved to compassion, placing my hand on her shoulder to comfort her. I asked her what was wrong.

She began to tell me the story of how she had just lost her husband and best friend of 25 years. They had worked 7 days a week at their family business for 20 years, saving and planning for the day they could retire and travel the world. One week after they sold the business and retired, he passed away suddenly and unexpectedly. She was at the store this day to pick out bedroom furniture to furnish a room at her daughter's house so she had a place to stay when things got tough for her.

"Customers are human beings."

As the face of the company or store where you work, you have the important job of interacting with customers. Customers are human beings. I believe we lose touch with this fact in the midst of all our training and focus on selling, product knowledge, policies and procedures. It's easy to lose sight of human beings with real problems, real issues, and real lives. Human beings who are happy, sad, upset, angry, suicidal, ecstatic, celebratory. Human beings with hopes and dreams. And as such, we first need to be prepared with the knowledge of how to interact with people, how to present ourselves, our product and our company with dignity and respect. During this process, we develop a genuine relationship with our customers, even if the relationship lasts no more than the length of time they are in the store. You never know when the kindness and respect you show your customer -- even that one handshake you extend to them -- may be the singular act of kindness they really needed. It's that process that builds customer loyalty and results in success for you and your company.

Real customer review

I had a fantastic experience shopping for an organic mattress with Nest Bedding. My husband and I wanted to get a latex mattress for his parents, and Joe Alexander was great at advising us on our purchase. He even talked me out of buying a mattress topper until after my in-laws tried out the mattress because the toppers are non-refundable. He clearly cared about our finances and didn't want us to spend money if we didn't need to. He also worked really hard to rush our mattress order, and kept us up to date by email with the status of our shipment. I just think that Joe offered stellar service, and I look forward to returning the next time I need a new mattress or other bedding.

My desire in writing this book is to share my nearly 30 years of successful selling skills. A major component of that process is deconstructing the retail experience to its most basic component: meeting people's needs and helping people solve their problems.

I hope that after reading this book you will find a new excitement and energy for your role in retail and you will begin to see your position through new eyes -- and your customers as the most valuable part of your job and your store. Happy selling!

Chapter 1 Building Retail Relationships

Do you know the names of your neighbors on either side of your residence? Across the street? When our country was still in its infancy, towns featured a communal square where their residents would come together for meetings and social gatherings. Fast forward to the present day, when you can't even have a conversation with a stranger because they are plugged into their music device or phone and have tuned out the world. More and more we are becoming compartmentalized and cut off from those around us and technologies that are intended to unite us are dividing us, and making us more anonymous to each other every day.

Growing up in the 1970s, before the advent of computer games and the era of the X-Box, the neighborhood kids and I gathered to play baseball, hide-and-seek and "ding-dong ditch'em" (email me and I will explain that one). These days you can drive endlessly down city streets and rarely see kids playing outside. We are more isolated, in terms of face-to-face interaction, from our neighbors than ever before. We prefer to meet in chat-rooms and interact via social networks, email and text messages.

A recent trip to New York had me taking the subway. The vast majorities of people were engaged with their mobile device or had their iPod or iPad as their companion. It has become an unusual event for your neighbors to knock on your door to introduce themselves or for a stranger to walk up to you and introduce themselves, but we have no problem "friending" the friend of a friend on the latest social network. We have severely limited our opportunities to interact face-to-face. One of the last bastions of human interaction is the retail experience. Shopping, in a very powerful way, has become the new town square.

"One of the last bastions of human interaction is the retail experience."

Human touch and interaction are as vital as food and water and yet, in this electronic age, where voicemail and online shopping dominate, we are finding less and less in person, face-to-face human interaction. Here is a good test: How many people have touched you today? If you are single and live alone, the answer is likely none: zero. And yet, touch -- as much as any other human sensory experience -- is a vital part of what we need to thrive as human beings.

Debra Moore, PhD, writes,

"We're all born with a great need for touch. To thrive, newborns must be fed touch as much as food. Studies in orphanages and hospitals repeatedly tell us that infants deprived of skin contact lose weight, become ill and even die. We know that premature babies given periods of touch therapy gain weight faster, cry less, and show more signs of relaxed pulse, respiration rate and muscle tension."

Enter the Retail Relationship. The retail experience has emerged as one of the few opportunities people have to interact with other people face-to-face. For many, shopping is the only time in their day they get to physically talk with other people outside of their workspace. Thus, we who work in sales -- in particular Retail Sales -- have the opportunity to take full advantage of this situation and make a friend of our customers. And trust me, it's much easier to make a sale when your customer sees you as a friend and not a salesperson. You may be the only person your customer interacts with face-to-face that day. When you shake your customer's hand, you may be the only person whom they touch all day. The exchange your customer has with you may be the only intimacy they experience over the course of their day.

Retail Relationships will teach you how to initiate and cultivate a relationship with your customers and in the process you will learn, from your customers, everything you need to know to help them make the decision to buy what you are selling. We will explore the face-to-face, interpersonal dynamics of relationships and relationship building, and discover how those dynamics apply to creating sales and customers who'll remember your name and their satisfying retail experiences with you and your products for life.

Real customer review

Thank you, thank you, thank you Joe. This was such a great experience. We were intrigued by the fascinating website. Had an informative telephone call with Joe. But the very best part was the fun we had pulling mattress layers and toppers out at the Nest Bedding store with Joe and trying to piece together the perfect bed for us. In fact it was so much fun; we ended up purchasing two beds. Joe is wonderful to work with, very knowledgeable and easy going. We love our two beds, are so very happy that we met Joe and tell EVERYONE we know that the Nest Bedding store, website and Joe are to be believed for the great service, [and the] truth in the product being sold and delivered that they provide.

"How can I help you?"

Quick! What is the first response that comes to your mind when you walk into a store and a salesperson asks you this question?

It's a question repeated millions of times in America every single day. You hear it upon entering retail stores throughout the country, and variations on it – in every conceivable language -- throughout the world. And it's about the most insincere and rude way to greet a potential customer. Yet companies big and small pay their staff to greet customers in this fashion. Corporations and Mom-and-Pop retail stores will spend valuable time and money training their staff on inventory, point-of-purchase procedures, store policies, store fixtures and advertising -- and hardly any resources on proper sales techniques. Basically, it's "Here is what you are selling, here is how to collect the money, now go sell." And without a plan and proper training, the store's sales staff will repeat that familiar mantra: "How can I help you?"

"I'm just looking."

When you board a train heading for a specific location, you really don't have grounds for protest when it delivers you to the announced location. The same goes for questions. It's comical when I hear salespeople getting upset with a customer who responds with "I'm just looking." when they were greeted with "How can I help you?" It's such a familiar routine that I would be surprised if you did not answer accordingly when I asked you to respond to the same question above.

Succinctly interpreted, this is what is being said when you greet a customer with the age-old, worn out "How can I help you?":

"I'm not interested in you but I want to sell you something so I can get a bigger paycheck or keep my job. What are you interested in buying?"

And the customer responds, "Yuck! A salesperson trying to sell me something! Get away from me! I will ask you a question when I am ready because you clearly are not interested in me as a person."

There is a lot going on behind those words. A struggle for control we don't even realize is taking place:

Salesperson: *"How can I help you?"* (I want to sell you something!)

Customer: *"I'm just looking."* (I don't want to be controlled or manipulated!)

Salesperson: *"What are you looking for?"* (I recognize that you don't want to talk to me, but I am going to disregard what you said and ask again.)

or

"Ok, let me know if you have any questions." (I give up control, but you let

me know when you are interested in talking to me again.)

While working for a mattress company as the General Manager, I not only managed our sales and marketing departments, but also managed and trained the retailers throughout the country who represented and sold our products. One afternoon I was in New York, visiting one of our retailers. It was my first face-to-face visit to the store and my goal was to train the store staff to sell our mattresses properly. The store was open on this brisk December day and while I was discussing the particulars of the construction of our mattresses with Diana (the store manager) a customer wandered in. The man was in his mid-20s, dressed very well and clearly on his way to work, perhaps on Wall Street. From her desk Diana cheerily lobbed those famous words across the expanse of the room without making an effort to get up:

"Hi, how can I help you?"

How did the very well-dressed, affluent-appearing young man respond? "Thanks, I am just looking." Then, to further seal her fate, Diana followed it up with about the worst possible, yet the one most commonly used:

"Let me know if you have any questions."

While Diana and I chatted about the specs and construction of the mattresses, the young man meandered about the store, pausing here and there. Within about 10 minutes, he circled back toward the front door and walked silently out into the brisk December morning and down the road, his wallet and any chance of him opening it in the store following him. I could only imagine that he had a no-limit American Express Platinum Card and a taste for the finer things, based on his attire and grooming. We'll never know.

The moment he walked out the door, I paused. "Diana, let's talk about what just happened here in your store. While we were speaking, your customer walked into the store and walked right out without saying a word to you, and you did not think it was rude. Nor did he. How would it make you feel if during our meeting I just stopped mid-sentence, gathered my things and without a word, walked out the door?" She thought about it a second and answered, "That would be really rude!" I replied, "Isn't it interesting that your customer just walked into the store and walked right out without a word and you did not think it was rude?"

Diana answered, "But I know you."

Did you ever walk down the street and have a total stranger ask you for money? If you live in a major metropolitan area, you have a built-in response to this because it happens often. My usual one, which is more often than not true, is, "Sorry, I don't have any cash on me." If panhandlers would get creative, they would get smartphones -- with a Paypal app -- so they could respond, "That's OK, I take credit cards and Paypal." But most people, like me, don't find it too difficult to say no to a stranger. The same dynamic takes place when the phone rings and there is a pre-recorded message, or a total stranger who launches into a quickly-spoken sales pitch. It's quite simple and often the most natural reaction to just hang up the phone.

Now let's say it's a co-worker or casual acquaintance who asks you for money. Is it harder to say no? Of course it is. Let's go a step further. Let's say it's your mother or father, brother, sister, child or spouse asking to borrow some money. See the trend here? It is much easier to say no to a stranger than it is to say no to a friend, acquaintance or someone who you know.

During the next 20 minutes I taught Diana how to properly greet customers, and on cue an older woman walked into the store. Diana stood up from the desk, approached in the manner in which I had instructed her, and using a script we had practiced said, "Hello, welcome to our store, have you been here before?" The woman matched Diana's smile, attitude and body language and enthused, "No, I haven't!" Diana executed the rest of the small script we had practiced and 30 minutes later, as the customer was preparing to leave, she stopped and hugged Diana. After the customer left, Diana excitedly came back to the desk, sat down and proclaimed:

"Why doesn't anyone teach us this stuff?"

Diana was well on her way to building healthy, happy, and successful Retail Relationships by never getting on the "I am just browsing" train.

Have you ever experienced stop-and-go traffic, bumper-to-bumper, and experience that one guy who pulls up right alongside of you with his turn signal on, trying to force his way into your lane in front of you? Unwilling to let this guy take your hard-earned position in the lane, you creep forward, preventing him from inserting the nose of his vehicle into your lane. Do you look over at him? NO WAY! The minute you make eye contact with him, you are doomed, and have to let him in.

Once you humanize the situation -- once you make eye contact -- you feel obligated to be nice and courteous. It's hard to be mean to someone with whom you have made eye contact. Just that little bit of intimacy can get you to lower your guard.

"It's hard to be mean to someone with whom you have made eye contact."

I can call my local hardware store on the phone and get their hours. I can go online and see what their inventory is before I go into the store. I can wander the aisles and never encounter a salesperson. And I can go to the self-checkout lane and never personally interact with a store employee. Taking into account the words of Dr. Moore at the outset of this book, and considering the example of what happened with Diana in New York or the guy trying to nudge his way into traffic, it's mind boggling that multi-million dollar corporations would dehumanize their entire customer interaction process. Do you have a favorite cash register at the self-checkout line that asks how your kids are? Does the recorded voice on the phone suggest a couple of other pieces of furniture that might go well with the sofa about which you are inquiring? You can't build a relationship with an inanimate object. You can't experience loyalty with the ATM machine. You're not able show pictures of your kids to the self-serve kiosk at the mall. We have, as a culture, taken technology and used it to replace the human experience, and we are so proud of our efficiency and ability to cut costs -- never considering the implications and how these practices affect our ability to form and sustain productive Retail Relationships.

Do you have a favorite hair stylist? Shoeshine guy at the airport? Sushi restaurant where the same person makes your favorite Alaska Roll the way they know you like it? Is there a Melissa at your home improvement store who smiles and says hi whenever you shop there? Chances are if you shop or visit the same stores repeatedly, over time you are going to establish relationships with the people you encounter. And you are going to continue to shop at those places because of those relationships. Why?

Human beings are, by nature, social creatures. We crave human interaction. We were designed with the ability and desire to communicate -- to interact with other human beings. We value and enjoy a sense of community and a sense of belonging. When we punish people as a society, we choose to take them away from a sense of community and we isolate them in prisons. This is in some sense the worst punishment, knowing that for any human being social interaction is a fundamental need and desire.

Psychiatrist Dr. Bruce Perry, when interviewed by the *San Diego Examiner* on the topic of Childhood Development, said:

"Humans are designed to be interdependent on others. So when infants and young children are cut off from a variety of social

interactions, their emotional and cognitive growth suffers. In fact, bringing in more social interaction can actually help children who have suffered a trauma."

Knowing this basic and fundamental information about how human beings are designed and function should influence how we communicate and conduct ourselves when working on the retail level. When we look at the customer as just a sale and just a means to an end -- as a means to profitability -- we craft a retail experience that is based on market efficiencies and cost-per-transaction but which is devoid of the genuine compassion and care people need to feel at their best and open to possibilities. Yet when we recognize that customers are human beings with feelings and needs, and that we are here to serve their needs and wants, it begins to radically alter our approach.

"When we recognize that customers are human beings with feelings and needs, and that we are here to serve their needs and wants, it begins to radically alter our approach."

Several years ago, I was asked by a local branch of the *Hispanic Yellow Pages* to give a seminar to help increase their sales. They were a business-to-business sales organization, with sales reps daily walking into small retail shops, uninvited and unannounced, with the intention of selling *Yellow Pages* advertising to the Hispanic community.

After spending a few days on the road with their sales staff and observing first-hand how they went about plying their craft, I was ready to help. I had management assemble their staff in their conference room and erect a large whiteboard at the head of the room. Addressing the assembled sales staff, I asked them to start blurting out their answers to this question:

"What are some of the words you would use to describe a business owner?"

They started shouting out terms like "hard charging", "tough," "independent," "mean," "rude" and "successful." After I filled an entire side of the board, I asked another question:

"Now, how about when I ask you to give me a word that describes salespeople?"

Keep in mind these are salespeople I am posing this question to, and yet the answers were hilarious and poignant. "Sneaky", "dishonest," "liars" and "pushy." No wonder they were having a hard time selling! They wouldn't even want to talk to *themselves,* let alone the store owners.

With both columns filled, I asked them a simple question; "What is the common denominator between these two groups? What is the common ground with which we can make a sale?" There was quite a bit of head-scratching and a few feeble attempts to find a common phrase, but no one answered correctly. It's OK -- it's rare anyone does.

I drew a line between both groups and wrote the word, "Human Being" on the board.

Chapter 2 From Stranger to Relationship

One of the toughest and most intimidating aspects of relationship building is initiating a conversation with a total stranger. It takes a great deal of self-confidence to approach someone you don't know, who may look, act and dress different than you, and make an introduction. Most of us are familiar with this dynamic from the dating world. We have all had experience either receiving or delivering a "pickup" line at a club, bar or social event. In retail it's really no different, as we are charged with initiating a conversation with a total stranger and facing rejection.

In the dating world, it usually falls to the men to initiate contact, so let's examine things from a male point of view. Men who are successful at approaching women follow these seven rules, as outlined at AskMen.com:

1- Make Eye Contact Before the Approach

2- Don't Express Interest in Both Her and Her Friends

3- Make Her Feel Like She's the Hottest Woman in the World

4- Don't Avoid Complimenting Her if You Think She's Heard It All Before

5- Don't Use Cliché, Pre-Packaged Pickup Lines

6- Approach Her in Places Other than Bars and Nightclubs

7- Know When to Walk Away

Let's not sugarcoat the reality: Regardless of gender, the way you might approach someone you are interested in dating is a similar dynamic to that which you encounter when selling. In both instances you have specific intentions: You are interested in genuinely getting to know the person and you intend to instigate a mutually beneficial relationship. In a dating situation, you want to get to know the other person and if you hit it off, you want to date with the intention of building a relationship. And in the Retail Relationship, building intimacy and trust will help your customer open up, trust you and like you, making it easier for you to uncover and meet their wants and needs -- thereby creating a mutually beneficial relationship.

"Building intimacy and trust will help your customer open up, trust you and like you."

If you are a super model, you would likely be more successful walking up to someone at a bar or club and just asking her or him out. For the rest of us, we would be more successful using the steps listed above. The same holds true for the retail experience. Walking up to a customer and stating "How can I help you?" is essentially the same as walking up to a customer and asking, "How can I take your money today?" You would likely meet with as much success as the average person trying to pick up a supermodel or ballplayer.

1- Make Eye Contact Before the Approach

Debbie Bailey of Trainer2Go Inc., author of *Look Em' in the Eyes: The Real Power of Eye Contact* gives a clear description of effective eye contact:

"Why is eye contact so powerful? Good eye contact cuts physical distance in half, helps you connect with your audience on a personal level, invites audience members to participate in your conversation, enables you to gauge your audience's reaction to your presentation, stops hecklers from pestering you, and so much more...

"There's an oft-quoted old English proverb that goes, "The eyes are the windows to the soul."

There's an oft-quoted old English proverb that goes, "The eyes are the windows to the soul." As Debbie points out, effective eye contact accomplishes a lot of objectives. Making eye contact with your customer ensures that you have their attention and creates a sense of intimacy with them. It's much easier to tell someone bad news or to be tough when they are not in front of you. But when they are right in front of you, making eye contact with you, you will find you are much more considerate and gentle. If you avoid eye contact with the customer, or don't encourage and welcome it from the customer, it will be much easier for them to reject and avoid you.

I inherited a seasoned sales staff at the furniture store I used to manage, and one of the salespeople on the staff -- we will call him "Bob" -- had been a salesperson with the company for 17 years. Bob was an amazing resource. He knew everything about every product from every affiliated company. If you needed to know if a certain sofa was available in a certain fabric, all it took was just to ask Bob. You would think with all that product information, Bob would be the best salesperson. However, it was the opposite. Bob had a very difficult time making eye contact with people. Looking over years' worth of sales information revealed that Bob was always at or near the bottom in sales every month. Watching him interact with customers, in particular during the introduction, was painful. You could see the customers visibly squirm and attempt to get away from Bob as soon as he started talking. Because his eyes darted all over the place, he gave customers the impression he was shifty and untrustworthy; a typical salesperson in the worst sense of the characterization.

It is not uncommon for some people to find it difficult to make eye contact; this is part of the human condition and is true for both customers and salespeople alike. If you are in sales and have a hard time making and maintaining eye contact, it is imperative to overcome this fear. Without the ability to make proper eye contact, you will simply not achieve a high level of success. The inability to make proper eye contact, in my experience, emanates from shyness and a lack of self-confidence.

"When you make proper eye contact while listening, it shows you are engaged and interested."

If you find yourself struggling with the ability to make eye contact with your customers, you are going to need to role play and practice. Recruit fellow salespeople or friends and family to help you. Eye contact does not mean you are staring into your customer's eyes -- it simply means you are connecting with your customer through healthy eye contact and speaking to them, not at them. When you make proper eye contact while listening, it shows you are engaged and interested.

So, what is effective time duration for a sales-healthy practice of making eye contact, and how can we achieve it? Lee Hopkins, managing director of Hopkins Business Communication Training and author of *Nonverbal Communication In Business*, says:

"So, here's a useful tip: break your eye-to-eye contact down to four or five second chunks. That is, look at the other person in blocks that last four to five seconds, then look away. That way they won't be intimidated. Practice timing yourself, away from others. Just look at a spot on the wall, count to five, and then look away. With practice, you will be able to develop a 'feel' for how long you have been looking into your audience member's eyes and intuitively know when to look away and focus on another person or object."

Mr. Hopkins suggests focusing on a spot on a wall for a few seconds, then looking away. You can also use a mirror to see yourself talk, pause, and look away.

Another effective technique I have utilized is making "soft" eye contact with customers. You can pick a spot very near their eyes without looking directly into them. This has helped some salespeople I have worked with overcome the eye-contact dilemma. The goal is to show confidence and empathy, not to bore holes through the customer's skull or win a staring contest.

Remember, eye contact is crucial to sales and imperative in those first few moments as customers are forming opinions about you and your intentions. If you find you are shy or self-conscious, you need to practice proper eye contact, but also create a new internal paradigm about how you see yourself. Be confident in your sales ability, and in the fact you are a nice, honest, trustworthy person with something worthwhile to sell. That confidence will help you remember your position is very important in the overall success of your company and in the customer's search to have their needs and wants met and their problems solved.

2- Don't Express Interest in Both Her and Her Friends

3- Make Her Feel Like She's the Hottest Woman in the World

4- Don't Avoid Complimenting Her if You Think She's Heard It All Before

What is the intent with steps 2-4? The intention is to make the subject feel special -- to make someone feel that you are sincerely interested in them as a human being. To show them you feel they are not just another person at the bar, but someone special.

In the retail setting, we do this by approaching the customer in a non-threatening manner, making eye contact, getting and using their name, shaking their hand and asking them questions to which we genuinely listen to the answers. We will get further into these techniques as this book progresses, but for now, know that if you treat the customer as just a sale, you will not, in any meaningful way, connect with the customer. People are very intuitive and sensitive, particularly in the retail setting where the negative stereotype of the pushy, insincere salesperson often prevails and the customer is on their guard against unwanted manipulation. They will know when you are being fake and insincere. Your words and your body language will tip them off to your intentions.

Speaking of negative stereotypes, what are some of the common indictments of salespeople? Remember the list the group at the *Hispanic Yellow Pages* gave when asked about salespeople? "Insincere," "rude," "pushy"? As a salesperson, you already have the deck stacked against you. Salespeople have a bad reputation -- and in that case, those were just salespeople evaluating other salespeople!

Just think what is running through the customer's head about you when you first approach. You can be the nicest, most sincere person in the world, but until the customer gets to know you, they are assuming you are something out of a nightmare, like "all the other salespeople" in the world.

At the bar you are just another person in the crowd trying to make a connection or pick someone up. When you show genuine interest and care enough to get to know the person, the person you are speaking with will see you as a genuine human being and lower their defenses. The same holds true in your store with your customers. When you approach and engage them on a human level, you are more likely to see the customer lower their defenses and have a conversation with you. When you approach with the typical "How can I help you?" you lump yourself into the group of stereotypical salespeople with which we all are familiar, and this will trigger your customer's defenses.

5- Don't Use Cliché, Pre-Packaged Pickup Lines

"How can I help you?" is a train that always leads to "I am just looking"-ville. It's about the worst destination at which you can arrive when greeting a customer. You rarely build real rapport with a customer that responds with the "I am just looking" reply.

"How can I help you?" is a throw-away line. It's trite and uncaring. It's a cliché, a pre-packaged pickup line. Some people use a variation of it that is even worse:

"How are you today? How can I help you?"

This is worse because they are asking an empty question with no intent of actually listening, caring or feeding back with how their customers are doing. Talk about conveying insincerity! And yet it's repeated daily by the majority of salespeople around the country. "How are you today?" We really don't want to hear the answer, so it becomes an impersonal greeting that leaves you sounding the worst way for a salesperson to sound: insincere. Interpreted, you just conveyed to your customer you don't care how they are, and you really mean, "Just tell me what you are looking for so I can sell you something and get on with my day with the least possible resistance."

It is so commonly used and abused, I have observed sales situations over and over again in which salespeople have approached customers with "How are you today?" and the customer has just begun telling them what they are looking for, completely oblivious to what the salesperson asked. Insincerity met with insincerity. And the saddest result is that you may or may not make a sale, but you certainly are less likely to make a customer and initiate a Retail Relationship.

6- Approach Her in Places Other than Bars and Nightclubs

To stick with the dating analogy, the intent behind this advice is acknowledging that good-looking women in bars or clubs are getting hit on constantly, so their guard is perpetually up and any potential suitors are less likely to be successful. This advice is relevant in our retail situation because we have to understand that when customers are coming into our store, their guard is similarly up. They are used to insincere salespeople, disinterested in them as human beings, just trying to sell them something, so their internal distrust meter (people of previous generations called this a person's "B.S. detector") is going to be on full alert when you -- a salesperson -- approach them. It's imperative to get on a different train if you want to arrive at a different destination. If you don't want "I'm just looking," I suggest you never get on the "How can I help you?" train because it always goes to the same unproductive, derelict station in the middle of nowhere. And once you go there, it's no fun and you're stuck on the "Island of No Sales."

So, what are some of the usual responses to "I am just looking"? We have all heard, "Let me know if you have questions," or "What are you looking for in particular?" These reflect the customer effectively telling you, "Stay away from me, you are a salesperson. I don't like salespeople and I don't want you trying to sell me something." Trying to engage the customer after they have told you "I am just looking" is pushy and defensive. Telling them to ask you questions if they need you is admitting defeat, gives the customer undue control, and it rarely results in sales. My advice? Watch the signals and just stay off this train altogether.

7- Know When to Walk Away

No one wants a pushy, insincere salesperson following them around the sales floor, particularly after they have asked to be left alone. Show of hands: How many people really enjoy going to car dealerships? If you raised your hand, it's because you are a car salesperson and have to go there for work! No one in their right mind wants to subject themselves to car salespeople. Why? They have the reputation of being vultures, swooping down and pushing you into a corner, trying to sell you something you don't want. I once had a store location situated directly next to a car dealership -- one with *terrible* online reviews. I often observed customers parking far away from view of the dealership and trying to creep onto the lot unnoticed, so they could see a car without being approached by sales staff. Understanding in context that you represent salespeople and people's perceptions of their interactions with sales staff as a whole will help you to understand how to approach customers in a more effective, successful fashion. A well-trained salesperson observes the verbal and nonverbal clues their customer is giving them so they'll know when to engage and when to give the customer some space. But the best part of building a Retail Relationship is that when executed properly, the techniques you will learn here will help the customer see you as a friend, an advocate and a trusted resource, and they will want you to stick around to meet their needs and solve their problems as they relate to the products you have on offer.

Real customer review

I talked with Joe, the owner, and he is very passionate about his store. He calls it his baby, spends 7 days a week on it, and is determined that his customers are happy with their purchase. When he heard of the problems I'd had, he apologized for not being able to talk to me personally that day, especially since his staff was still new. The staff are friendly, the products are quality, and the owner seriously makes his customers a top priority. How can you not be a fan?

Far too often I see salespeople dismiss customers because they misinterpret clues from the customer. Unless the customer asks for a few moments alone or gives you very clear nonverbal clues that they need space, don't leave!

When practiced properly, the Retail Relationship style will include you as a part of the decision-making process and not just a salesperson selling something. And if you do need to give them space, don't go far and don't get too engaged with other activities or the customer may interpret your actions as non-interest -- that you are too busy to be bothered. Busy yourself with mundane activities like straightening shelves or dusting nearby, always within view, and watch for nonverbal cues to re-engage the customer. Those clues can include actions such as the customer folding their arms, looking around, reading sales materials, or walking away from the item.

Know thyself

One of my hobbies is acting, and whenever I get the opportunity I will audition for a role in a movie or TV show filming in my area. Recently, I worked on a film co-starring Joaquin Phoenix. He was playing the role of a mean cuss -- a real curmudgeon -- and as most great actors, he was walking around the set between scenes in character. He had a scowl on his face, did not make eye contact with anyone and looked fierce, just like the character he was playing. And though he is one of my favorite actors, there was no way I was going to approach him in that state!

Great actors prepare for a role. They research, develop and study the mannerisms and speech patterns of the character they are portraying in order to be more believable. Sales is much the same. We need to prepare ourselves for being "onstage" and performing for our customers. We are more effective when portraying a confident, focused, intelligent and empathetic salesperson. But the fact is we are not a confident, focused, intelligent and empathetic salesperson every day. Some days we get up on the wrong side of the bed, maybe feeling under the weather or just we find ourselves distracted with cares and concerns in our lives. It's on those days we need to get into character and remember the fact our customers expect our best performance. This could be termed "bringing your best self to work."

A truly great sale begins with you, the salesperson. It consists of obvious hygienic concerns -- taking care of yourself physically by practicing proper and appropriate grooming, choosing the right clothing and having fresh-smelling breath. But it also encompasses having a good attitude and perspective. What you think about affects your actions. If you are distracted by cares and concerns outside the sales floor, regardless of where you are you are not at your best, and will of course not be able to bring your best self to work.

Each sales day you need to get into the habit of preparing not only your appearance but your mind and attitude. I find creating a checklist of things I have going on in my life is effective for helping me focus on work. I go down the list and write a plan of action for each concern and when I reach the bottom of the list, I have a clear plan for taking care of what needs to be taken care of, leaving my mind free to focus on customers and making sales.

Great salespeople have a great attitude -- a winning attitude. There is a difference between a cocky salesperson and a confident salesperson. No one likes a cocky, bragging, self-absorbed salesperson. But a confident salesperson is one to be emulated and admired.

I have always related a proper selling attitude to a professional baseball hitter. The Major League Baseball Hall of Fame in Cooperstown, New York enshrines hitters who completed their long careers achieving impressive milestones, one of which is hitting over .300 for their career. What does hitting .300 or better mean? It means they failed to hit successfully 70% of the time! Failing 70% may not sound great, but in baseball -- a game of precision -- it's impressive to ONLY fail 70% of the time.

Now, does this mean that a .300 hitter strides to the plate with the attitude of a 70% failure? No. A great hitter visualizes their successful at-bat before they come up to the plate and as they stand in to face the pitcher, they visualize themselves hitting the ball successfully every time. Does it mean they will hit it safely every time? Of course not. But successful people maintain a successful attitude, and recognize why it is necessary for outcomes of success, each and every time.

I personally believe I can sell anyone every time, because I believe I am one of the best salespeople you will ever meet. Cocky? No, just confident in my abilities. Do I really think I will sell everyone every time? Realistically, I know not everyone is ready to buy when I want them to buy, so I have to give them space to make the decision when they are ready. But I approach every customer with a winning, successful attitude, as that will always affect my actions and give me a better chance of making more sales. To be a successful salesperson, start seeing yourself as one and believing in your abilities.

A positive, successful attitude is a choice. There are circumstances in all our lives which -- if we allow them to -- will distract us, bring us down and mire us in negativity. However, I have found in my life that success and positivity is a choice based on a conscious decision to not allow anything to keep you from the success you want to achieve. One saying I live by is:

"The glass is not half empty or half full, it's 100% full, half air and half water."

It illustrates that a successful, positive attitude looks at things a little differently and sees the positivity in any circumstance, and that this is a conscious choice. With a successful, positive attitude you are ready to sell and build a successful Retail Relationship.

Chapter 3 Know Thy Customer

Now that we have prepared ourselves to sell, we need to know our customers and understand what they are dealing with and what they are thinking when they walk into our store or selling space.

Although I do not equate selling with warfare, it can be a very valuable analogy to equate a successful battle with a successful sale. A quick study of the most successful generals in history reveals they never went into battle without a tremendous amount of preparation – that is, detailed and intimate intelligence about their enemy -- and never, ever without a considered plan of attack. No surprises, no chances, nothing left to guessing. To do so would be to plan to fail. As salespeople, we would be foolish to not take the time to understand our customers, to walk in their shoes, and to look through their eyes so that we can effectively help them get their needs and wants met at our store, by us. So, let's step into our customers' shoes and begin to see our world through their eyes.

I have been selling, teaching sales, or running a sales team for almost 30 years. That's a lot of sales experiences. When I say I have seen or heard just about every category of customer out there, I am speaking from a perspective of experience. As of the writing of this book, besides teaching sales, I run a chain of mattress stores. And regardless of my role, I always want to be out with the customers, helping them one-on-one, so I can set an example for my staff, earn their respect, model proper techniques, and stay intimately in touch with what customers are wanting and the interactions and outcomes they are experiencing in my stores.

Of course, mattress sales has its challenges, right up there with car sales. On the list of most hated salespeople, mattress salespeople have to be near the top. With confusing marketing, balloons and other off-putting decorations at discount sales -- as well as the ever-present fear of haggling and negotiating and the fact that sleeping is a necessity and good, restful sleep an extremely necessary and valuable part of life – makes shopping for a mattress an often painful experience. Consumers just assume they are going to get ripped off, but come to the transaction fed up with the poor sleep their existing mattress provides and end up overpaying for something uncomfortable that won't last very long, in an effort to make *some* improvement to their sleeping conditions. Anyway, when it comes to balloons-as-decoration, I often say that if they are present at the purchase you are contemplating, run! I have seldom seen balloons associated with anything other than a store trying to get me excited about spending a lot of money unnecessarily.

I note my experience to make this point: What customers are often feeling when they walk through your store's door is fear: they are in fear of you, in fear of overspending, in fear of their needs and wants going unfulfilled and their problems unsolved, in fear of being taken advantage of, in fear of not getting a good deal, in fear of being less than knowledgeable on the items for sale, and in fear of being put on the spot and forced to make a decision.

In addition to all the fear racing around in their heads and hearts, there is usually a cavalcade of visual and audible stimuli that serves, in the customer's vulnerable state, to overwhelm them. One of the very first things I do when training a new salesperson is to have them walk outside with me and stand outside the door of our location. I have them close their eyes and listen to all the different sounds around them, to note the volume of the noises outside the door. Then I ask them to look around and tell me all the signs they see, all the marketing messages vying for their attention. I have them note the temperature and the smells, and then I have them walk through the doors of our store.

"The more expensive your product, the less

they know about your product,

and the less they know you, the more fear

exists for the customer."

Customers experience fear when contemplating a new purchase and entering an unfamiliar environment. If you think about it, most of our decision-making is born out of fear. We lock our houses for fear of attack or break-in. We buy organic produce for fear of chemical exposure. We look both ways when crossing the street for fear of getting hit by a car. We ask lots of questions out of fear of making a bad choice. Making decisions based on fear are not necessarily a bad thing, but it is very important to understand the dynamics your customer is grappling with when you are asking them to purchase with so much fear present. See it through their eyes, from the perspective of someone searching for what is yet unknown for them: the more expensive your product, the less they know about your product, and the less they know you, the more fear exists for the customer. And when you sell with fear still present, you are likely not to complete a sale or, if you do make the sale, you greatly increase your probability of a return, or a customer you will never see again, or even an unhappy customer. In this age of social networking – where the distance between your storefront and one of the many online sites where customers review, often negatively, commercial businesses is a mere click of a mouse away -- you simply *cannot* afford to have an unhappy customer.

So here is the picture: Our poor customer, riddled with fear, overwhelmed by sounds and messages, walks through the door of our store. It's no wonder they want to be left alone when we greet them with an insincere greeting!

When I take my new salesperson outside and let them get accustomed to what the customer is seeing, hearing, feeling and smelling, I have them walk through the door. Immediately there is a change in the temperature, in the sound level, in the brightness, in the messages. Going from a loud, bright environment to a cool, quiet and unknown environment can be daunting for a customer. Ever sit and watch customers come through the door of your store? If it's a big retail outlet, they likely cruise right in without hesitation. However, the smaller, more intimate your store, the more the customer feels trepidation, and more of a feeling they are onstage and the center of attention.

It's funny to observe these more intimate settings; because you can see customers enter slowly and cautiously, trying to avoid making eye contact. Conversely, when a confident and effective salesperson comes in, they walk right through the door as if they own the place. There is no fear because they are not buying anything. More than anything, customers fear being put on the spot; effective salespeople should not. With all the thoughts and emotions a customer is dealing with, the last thing we want to do is overwhelm them and push them further away.

One of my favorite analogies to illustrate this scenario is to liken it to approaching a dog. Let's say for a moment your job was to go door-to-door and place fliers on doorknobs. The first house you approach has an open yard with no fence, and there is an old dog on the stoop. As you approach, the dog wags its tail and rolls over, exposing its belly to you. Are you afraid? Of course not. You are likely to reach down and pet the dog, as it poses no threat. You go to the next house, which is surrounded by a low fence with a sign affixed to the gate warning you to "Beware of Dog." You enter cautiously and a dog comes racing around the corner of the house, barking loudly, rushing you with its hair standing up on its back, ears back and teeth bared. Are you going to go right up to that dog and pet it? Not unless you value your fingers!

Why is the dog approaching you in this manner? It's common knowledge that animals, when feeling threatened, will try to push the threat away with aggressive displays such as growling and barking. The hair on a dog's back raises up, to make themselves look bigger and more menacing. They bare their teeth to show their weapons and bark to scare the threat off. You would be a fool to try to approach such a dog in the usual manner, exhibiting the characteristics of fear.

The only way you should approach a dog like this is to display non-threatening body language and a soft voice. You need to convey to the dog that you mean it no harm. How do you do this? First, you lower your body to their level to look smaller, less menacing. Then you open your hands and offer them toward the dog -- low, so the dog can see them. Then you talk in softer, gentler and slower words and tones to soothe the dog, making no sudden movements or loud noises. You smile and tilt your head, taking on the body language that conveys that you are approachable. Only then will the dog start to relax and feel comfortable in approaching you. I guarantee you, were you to walk right up to that barking, snarling dog and loudly greet it, you would likely end up being bitten, and perhaps even being eaten alive!

Your customer is experiencing a very similar feeling: fear. Their body language is much like the dog's, in that they are trying to be protective and push you away. How often do you observe your customer turn their shoulder toward you or fold their arms tightly across their chest, avoiding eye contact, or even turning their back to you? And just like approaching the dog when it's in fear, you would be foolish to not acknowledge your customer's fear when approaching them. Be careful -- you don't want to get bitten!

Real customer review

We'd been bed-shopping for awhile and, despite our state of sleep deprivation, were not too eager to face a blizzard of hyper-enthused bed salesmen. Then my girlfriend remembered running into Joe at work one day. He said he was opening a new store in Albany, offering organic and chemical-free beds and bedding at fair prices. We really wanted to support local small business, if we could afford to do so, and, after visiting his website, we decided to see Joe. There was no sales pitch, he was just a friendly person who knew all about beds and had passionately created a beautiful little business selling them.

Now that we have a clear understanding of what our customer is dealing with before we ever encounter them, knowing they are experiencing fear, knowing they distrust salespeople, knowing they are not acclimated to your sales environment -- knowing all of this information, we can start to craft a battle plan to effectively reach our customer and make not only a sale, but a healthy, successful Retail Relationship.

Step 1: The greeting

"You never get a second chance to make a first impression."

This simple, well-known axiom rings true and illustrates quite simply that a first impression is set in stone. People make very quick judgments about whether they are going to like and trust you based on immediate observations of your behavior and appearance. These observations include your dress, your countenance, your attitude, capacity for eye contact, your body language, tone of voice, choice of words and other factors. As the saying goes, once you make that first impression, it sets the foundation for everything that follows. Your customer filters every word and gesture through the filter of how they feel about you – perceptions largely created by their first impressions of you. Since the first impression sets the tone for the entire sale, let's go through this list and talk a bit about each one of these factors.

Appearance

You are walking home, late at night, lost. You make a turn down a deserted alley. You hear a bottle break and then menacing, foreboding laughter. You turn around and three large men are following you. Dressed like thugs in black clothing and ski masks, you immediately make a judgment about your situation. You don't need to spend the next half-hour taking in your surroundings to know that you need to hightail it out of there. Now, the guys could be three buddies coming home from a costume party, innocently enough. But in that heightened state of fear, being lost in the proverbial dark alley, you are on high alert.

Now, in the same alley and in the same circumstances, you hear a bottle break only to turn and find a family dressed like they are coming home from church with their kids. You immediately discern no threat because they do not appear to be menacing. It doesn't take us but a split second to make observations and subsequent judgments, whether they are right or wrong, and act accordingly. As we noted before, our customers are already in that heightened state of fear, so we need to ensure we are giving them the first impression of someone who is there to help, not to hinder or attack them. So, according to basic human nature, the first thing customers observe from a distance when they enter our store is our attire.

Wearing the appropriate attire for our profession is vitally important to our customer's evaluation of us. It is comical to me every time I step on a retail floor and see a salesperson in a suit or shirt and tie. Now, if I am selling insurance, real estate, or Mercedes-Benz cars, or if I am representing my company to another company, a suit or shirt and tie is very appropriate. But in a retail setting where your clientele is normal, average, everyday people, you are immediately conveying through such formal dress that you are formidable and what you are selling is expensive. Not exactly the first impression that is going to put your customer at ease.

The opposite of wearing a suit or shirt and tie would be to under-dress. Conveying to the customer you don't care enough to iron your shirt, or wearing shorts while selling a high-end item on a high-end sales floor is unwise. Your customer will quickly surmise that you are not someone who appears to be trustworthy or even remotely serious.

What is the appropriate attire, then? It depends on a few factors. First of all, look at your target market -- your ideal customer -- and try to dress similarly to them. If you are selling mattresses or furniture, you should dress "business casual" or in a company uniform. This conveys to the customer that you are professional or part of a team of professionals, and have been trained to help them. Dress too fancy, and the customer feels they are going to spend too much. Under-dress and they won't be inclined to trust or respect you.

The same would apply to personal grooming. To be taken seriously, you will want to maintain good grooming habits. This means neatly styled hair and facial hair for men, with a minimum of jewelry for both men and women -- and limited exposed piercings or tattoos. I am not opposed to them and have seen great salespeople with tattoos or piercings, but in general have found it's better to keep them covered or downplayed.. Remember, you want to be taken seriously and this means you want to avoid aspects of your attire becoming a distraction.

One Halloween in Hawai'i, our boss told us we could dress up for the holiday. I chose to dress up as a skater punk, complete with a skateboard and fake scars. I watched as customer after customer I greeted recoiled at the sight of me. Once they understood, they acted OK, but I did not make a single sale that day. I was asking for their trust but I did not appear worthy of it.

Body Language

I have had the privilege of learning the importance of body language and its role in sales from one of the foremost body-language experts in America, Ms. Jan Hargrave. Jan has coached some of the most influential people and companies in the world on how to use and interpret body language to achieve success.

Jan's book, *Strictly Business Body Language,* is a must-read for anyone who is engaged in business and sales. In it, Jan teaches that the overwhelming majority of what we say to a customer is never conveyed with words. That's right: the old saw about 75% of communication being nonverbal is true – and most of what we say and convey to a customer is done non-verbally. This really surprises people the first time they hear it, primarily because everything they have been taught, or teach, is so focused on the words and content with a focus on presentation skills. Words are important for sure, but if you are telling your customer with your body language that you are unsure of yourself or you are not confident in what you are saying – or that you're lying -- the words you are using will likely fall on deaf ears. The customer could leave after telling you they will be back, and you could think you gave a great presentation, yet all the while they never believed a word you said because your body language was betraying the very words you were using.

Jan's book goes into great detail about body language: how to use it and how to interpret it, which is very good information and vital to successful selling. Even more important is that first impression. I will go into more depth later in the book, but for our first impression, we are going to approach our customer much like we would approach that barking, snarling dog with its teeth bared: hands low and open as you approach, then up into a steeple gesture (more on this later), walking slowly, smiling, head slightly to the side, eyebrows raised and making eye contact.

When the customer sees a nicely dressed professional approaching in a non-threatening manner, and makes slow, deliberate gestures that are not conveying an attack, the customer discerns that the salesperson is not a threat and they can relax.

How important is it that you convey proper body language? According to Alton Barbour, author of *Louder Than Words: Nonverbal Communication*, the total impact of a message breaks down like this:

7 % -- verbal (words)

38 % -- vocal (volume, pitch, cadence, etc.)

55 % -- body movements (mostly facial expressions)

That is, a whopping 93% of what we are saying is non-verbal! Do you spend 93% of your time working on the nonverbal or 93% of your time working on your presentation and closing techniques? The value and impact of unspoken communication is beyond our ability to estimate or quantify it.

One of my favorite stories about body language comes from when I was living in Hawai'i, working for a high-end dating service company. The owners and I went shopping for a nice desk for my new office, to a high end European furniture manufacturer's showroom in Honolulu. When we walked through the doors, there was an older gentleman behind a desk. Upon seeing us, he did not bother to get up out of his chair. Instead, still seated, he threw his hands up in front of himself, waving them like we were backing up a 16-wheel semi into a family of ducks crossing the street. You would have thought we were physically attacking him!

He said, in a loud tone:

"You probably just want to be left alone, so feel free to wander around."

Really? No, we were actually looking for a desk, and had he gotten up off his butt and greeted three professionally-dressed, affluent-looking customers, we may have bought one from him. Instead, we spend about three minutes in the store, laughing out of sheer disbelief that a company would allow such odd and counterproductive behavior from its sales staff.

I recently had one of my salespeople approach a customer with our sales script, verbalized perfectly. However, the salesperson walked at an overly fast pace, speaking very quickly and loudly. The front door area is a bit cramped, which also can contribute to a customer feeling trapped if the salesperson comes across too "big," making the customer feel pinned and blocked-in. The customer, observing the body language, recoiled from the salesperson and literally said,

"I feel like you are going to slap me!"

Not the kind of first impression you want to make. Needless to say, the customer never relaxed and bought nothing. However, the customer did say something very important, beginning with the crucial "I feel..." They did not even hear a word the salesperson said, all they "heard" was the salesperson's body language, which made them "feel" attacked and turned off.

Another key component of body language is your face and facial expression. A smile is vitally important when greeting someone and helping them see you as friendly, approachable and non-threatening.

Dale Carnegie, in his famous book *How to Win Friends and Influence People,* talks about the importance of smiling in making friends:

Your smile is a messenger of good will. Your smile brightens the lives of all who see it. To someone who has seen a dozen people frown, scowl or turn their faces away, your smile is like the sun breaking through the clouds. Especially when that someone is under pressure from his bosses, his customers, his teachers or parents or children, a smile can help him realize that all is not hopeless -- there is joy in the world.

Not only does smiling convey these virtues to your customer, you have to keep in mind that you are selling. The fundamental element that I teach all salespeople is the reality that they are selling themselves. Customers need to buy you before they will buy anything you are selling them. And they make a quick decision, based on the factors we are discussing, if they are going to buy you.

If you appear happy, confident, successful, well-dressed and groomed, likable and non-threatening, customers will buy you, they will believe you, and they will buy into whatever it is you are selling.

I have seen this at work time and time again, and as recently as just yesterday. I had a young couple in the mattress store, and after selling them their new mattress, they began discussing their need for new furniture with me. They started asking me my opinion of certain brands, and even asked me to accompany them down the street to a rival mattress store to see the bedroom furniture they were considering. Now, they have mattresses and mattress salespeople at that mattress store. Why didn't they buy a mattress there? Why didn't they trust the salesperson's opinion in that store? Obviously they trusted me over him. They "bought" me. If you are happy, confident, and successful, customers will want what you have and act accordingly.

A simple truth of life and living is that we get what we give. When you exude friendly, non-threatening body language that conveys confidence and caring, the customer will like you, letting down their guard and trusting you. That is the foundation on which you can build a solid Retail Relationship and make a customer.

Again, I encourage you to practice, with co-workers, family or in front of a mirror. Observe yourself, your expressions, your smile. Would you find yourself approachable?

Quieting your Body

When it comes to communicating physically, there are a myriad of different things your body, your facial expressions, your posture and your actions can convey to a customer. Instead of trying to master every one of them, I teach a technique called *Quieting your Body*. Quieting your body simply means that we limit body language to just a few simple actions so we are careful not to negate or confuse what we are trying to communicate to the customer or distract them from our message. And we certainly don't want to give them the impression we are not being honest or that we are not trustworthy by not conveying proper body language. For example, we can be completely sincere but have our hands behind our back, not realizing we are making the customer feel we are hiding something. Or, we could be rubbing our face with our hands and not realize we are unconsciously conveying dishonesty.

Quieting our body limits our movements on the sales floor to just a few proven and powerful expressions and prevents us from sending mixed messages. The movements and practices we use in quieting our body are as follows:

1. Steepling: Hands forming a steeple, relaxed and mid-torso (as in fig. 1) when speaking and low and relaxed when listening.

(fig. 1 Steepling while speaking.)

2. Hands low, open and exposed, upon greeting and while speaking. (fig. 2)

(fig. 2 -- hands low, opened and inviting)

3. Smile!

That's it, very simple. These three movements constitute the quieting your body technique, which ensures you are not clouding up the conversation with too many messages. This menu of body language movements conveys confidence, openness and trust. As you start to learn steepling, you will start noticing on TV and in public settings how often those in the spotlight use steepling techniques. You can tell they have been well-trained.

One of the competitors in our local market acts as his own spokesman on their company television commercials. It is almost painful to watch as he uses body language that conveys a message of distrust and deception as he hides his hands and places his hands behind his back..

It's not always easy to change, or present our best self -- we all have default body language. A default is what we do when we are not paying attention. Like walking into your bathroom at home and flipping on the light switch. Unless you just moved in today, you don't need to stop and look for the light switch. You have flipped it on so many times you don't even think about it -- you do it unconsciously. It's a default, an automatic. Steepling will feel awkward at first because it is not your normal default. By practicing it, however, it will become your new default, so when you are talking with your customers you will do it without thinking and begin to reap its benefits in sales.

3. Tone and cadence of your voice, and the words you use.

Now that we have laid the proper foundation to engage the customer, we don't want to mess it up by opening our mouth and uttering the wrong thing. After 30 years, you can imagine I have heard my share of salespeople talking their customer right out of a sale. And not just with the words they use, but with their volume, intonation and cadence.

I was training a new salesperson one afternoon, and after several role playing sessions, I determined he was ready to try a live customer. In walked a couple that happened to consist of two women. He walked right up and said:

"How are you guys doing today?"

Now, it was very plain that these were not guys. Even though that is a common term for addressing people, it is far, far from professional. Talk about insulting! And of course, he was not able to recover and the couple left not long after. He was not able to establish any rapport with them -- imagine that. Their body language the entire time was that of dislike and disdain, completely closed off, arms folded. They behaved as if they had been subtly insulted, and they had been. No one is going to buy anything from anyone they don't like or whom they perceive has insulted them. It is therefore imperative to use gender-neutral words when greeting customers, and keep to a simple, succinct script. A practiced script ensures we default to proper verbiage and keep the sales interaction in a potential Retail Relationship on track.

In conversations with salespeople and through my own observations, I have seen many salespeople go all over the map with their greetings, using different approaches based on their own first impressions of the customer. They can incorrectly assume the customer does not have money or is not really seriously interested in buying. This (often erroneous) belief will influence your tone, your body language and your enthusiasm, and customers will pick up on your insincerity. You can demonstrate this by closing your eyes and imagining walking on a train track. Easy enough, right? Now let's take that train track and stretch it between two 20-story buildings.

How would that make you feel to have to walk across that track now? A little shaky? The idea of falling would affect your actions; you likely would not walk across with the same speed and confidence, instead being much more deliberate and careful. Your thoughts and your beliefs in situations always affect your body language.

No story I know of illustrates this point more effectively than one that took place one evening several years ago, when I was a sales manager at a furniture store near a major university in California. Being located in a college town meant that once a year we would get an influx of students looking to furnish their dorms or apartments. The store stocked furniture priced a bit out of the range of college students, and since we operated on an "up" system, -- a carousel of rotating salespeople that take turns as customers enter -- no salesperson wanted to waste their "up" on a student.

This particular evening a young lady walked into the store. She definitely did not look like the type of girl who looked like she had much money, and my staff responded in kind by disappearing into the bowels of our cavernous showroom. They looked at the lady's appearance and quickly surmised she was not going to buy. This angered me, particularly because this was one issue that I made clear to my staff I would not tolerate: No cherry-picking! It's rude to customers and to your fellow salespeople.

Anyway, since no one wanted to help her, I approached and greeted her. Within a few moments a young man came in and joined her. During our conversation I found out the young man was her brother and he was buying her a desk and bedroom furniture for her dorm room. They were the nicest kids and I enjoyed their company, and a nice little commission on a slow night, not to mention the chance to show my staff the error of their wrongly-assumptive ways.

I make it a habit of walking all my customers to their cars, and when we got to the parking lot these particular people were driving a brand new $90,000 Porsche. The young man told me that he had recently sold his software company to Microsoft for 30 million dollars. A few weeks later, on a busy Saturday, I was paged to the front of the store by one of the salespeople who had blown off the siblings that night.

They were back with their parents. The brother said he had just bought his folks a new house and wanted me to fill it with furniture. My staff stood around gawking as they spent tens of thousands of dollars. What's the lesson here? Never change your plan based on your observations of a customer. Just assume everyone who walks in the door is there to buy. Remember, no one goes to McDonald's to look at the menu. Greet every customer with the same respect, enthusiasm and sincere smile.

Of course, it's not fair to always pick on my staff without throwing myself under the bus as well. Yes, I really blew it on one particular occasion:

I once worked in a retail store that was situated near a retirement community. Fancying myself Mr. Personality, whenever we had elderly customers come in the door I frequently greeted them with a playful tone, addressing them as "kids." Most of the time, they laughed and had fun with it. However, one afternoon, I did this with an elderly gentleman who was deeply offended that I called him a kid and expressed his displeasure to me with "both barrels blazing." I felt foolish as he turned on his heels and walked right out the door, got in his car and left. My company spent good money to attract that customer, only to have me chase him right out the door. A properly trained sales staff is the lifeblood of any company. Remember: nothing happens in a company until somebody sells something. And as such, a poorly trained sales staff can sink a company.

The tone of your voice, its volume and its cadence play an important role in your customer forming a great first impression. Much like the story of the attacking dog earlier, you don't want to come across as hostile or aggressive when first approaching your customer. One common rookie mistake I see salespeople make is once they are trained and start taking their first customers, they are so excited to try out their new tools that they speak too fast and overwhelm their customers, coming across as attacking or overbearing. Earlier, we discussed the customer's experience when walking through the front door, and all the sensory information they are dealing with when they enter the store. As we learned earlier in the book *Louder Than Words: Nonverbal Communication*, 38% of communication is vocal (volume, pitch, cadence, etc.). In a large portion of what we communicate, we do so with the tone and timing of how we say what we say.

When a rookie salesperson approaches a customer and talks too fast, the customer cannot track what the salesperson is saying and will usually respond with either "What?" or they will just start asking questions, completely disregarding whatever the salesperson had said. All of the elements we are learning in this book are dependent on the other person, and here we see two of them at work: eye contact and slow, clear speech.

At the onset of the greeting, ensure the customer can follow what you are saying by making eye contact and slowing down your speech. One without the other negates both, and it is ineffectual to start a greeting before making eye contact. An effective way to get someone to make eye contact with you is to start your greeting with a slightly elevated volume on the first word, then continuing with your slow, gentle tone and cadence. A loud noise gets people's attention. The louder voice will draw the customer's attention, and once you have initiated eye contact, you can effectively communicate with your customer.

Another very common mistake I see salespeople making is the excessive use of "Um's" and other awkward, verbalized pauses when speaking with a customer. Such inflections are not what you want to hear when you are lost. "Um" – or other verbal placeholders of indeterminacy -- are not what you want to hear when you ask your spouse if they love you. "Um" is not what you want to hear when you ask your doctor if you are indeed going to live past next Thursday. And "Um" is not what you want to hear from someone when you want help. "Um" is not the reassuring and galvanizing language used by leaders and experts. Listen to people like President Barack Obama give a speech, or someone else in authority speak. You will rarely hear them say "Um..." while they are delivering their message.

Removing "Um" from your vocabulary is vital if you want to be taken seriously and be seen as a leader. Great speakers learn to pause when they are searching for a word or between thoughts. Saying "Um" makes it appear you don't know something and don't know what to say. But pauses between thoughts cause you to speak slower, more deliberately and sound more authoritative. Eradicating "Ums" and replacing them with less interrupting, flow-destroying pauses is a learned behavior and will take work. I recommend working with another person, family member or co-worker with role playing to practice effective, appropriate pausing. Understand that removing "Ums" from your vocabulary will pay big dividends in your sales career, and in general people will take you more seriously.

Chapter 4 Lead or Follow?

Now that we have explored the dynamics of those first few moments of the sale and exposed the inadequacy of the common greeting, it's time to discuss constructing a professional, succinct and effective greeting in its place. What we want to accomplish is to create an environment where we are leading the customer from the very first moment they walk in the door. Basically, we are showing the customer they do not have to lead -- that we are the expert and we will lead them. That they are, to paraphrase insurance giant Allstate, in the best possible hands.

There are plenty of opinions out there about how to approach a customer, but what I teach has worked for me in several different sales environments and works very well in a retail environment. As far as I am concerned, this simple script is worth the price of this book because by implementing it or a variation of it, you will increase your overall sales simply by setting the proper foundation for the successful outcome.

The script I will teach you is based upon a simple premise:

Whoever asks the questions is leading the conversation.

I am of the conviction that 99.9% of the world is comprised of followers, and there are precious few true leaders in this world. At one time or another we are all lost, whether if it's in seeking spiritual enlightenment, trying to find an address, putting together a desk from IKEA or wondering what path to take in our life. In these moments, when we are unsure or uninformed, we look to be led by a guiding light -- someone informed and confident to take our hand and show us the solution to our problem.

Before the proliferation of GPS devices, when you were lost a "positioning satellite" consisted of some guy on the side of the road you would ask for directions. If the person hesitated, hemmed and hawed – obviously guessing as to which way to tell you to go -- you would quickly dismiss them and not dare go where they suggested. You would find and ask someone else and if they confidently pointed you in the right direction, you would go where they led you. Why? Because you don't know where you are and that last person sounded like they knew what they were talking about. They sounded confident.

Back in 2004, I heard Barack Obama speak at the Democratic National Convention. I looked over at a friend and stated, "That will be our next President." This was long before President Obama was even on the radar as being a potential contender for that lofty position. Why did I say this? Because public confidence in President George W. Bush had drastically waned and the general public was hungry for a leader -- someone in whom they could put their trust. Obama sounded cool, confident and spoke with a steady, measured voice. He was eloquent. He conveyed proper body language. A couple of years later he was elected President by the largest margin of the modern political era. Four years later, he was re-elected by a substantial margin of victory. All this serves to illustrate my premise that when people are lost, they show that they are looking for a leader. If you aren't a leader, you are not part of the solution. When you exude confidence, customers will buy into you whether you're trying to get their votes in an election or you're trying to sell them a mattress or some other product.

One summer I worked on a car lot, and I quickly identified a trait consistent with the top-producing salespeople on the lot: the top producers' customers would follow them, and the non-producers were led around the lot by their customers. And I never once saw a customer lead a salesperson to the cash register.

A leader takes control. A leader asks the questions. A leader speaks slowly, deliberately, clearly and authoritatively so the customer can understand their words and digest their meaning. A leader takes the customer by the hand and leads them to the solution to their problem. A leader does not use "Um" between sentences -- they pause. I cannot tell you how happy I was every time I had a customer walk into my mattress store in Hawai'i with the business card of another salesperson from another store with a bunch of specs on the back, asking if I carried a similar product. I recognized what this was: A customer who was lost, and who had been driven away by a salesperson that did not take their hand and lead them confidently to their solution. That type of customer was an easy sale every time. That customer just wanted to buy a solution to their issue, and no one was showing it to them. Those other salespeople were too busy giving the customer information and specifications, leaving the customer to interpret the facts and decide for themselves if those facts and specs would add up to solving their problem. When I led, they bought.

With a clear understanding of leading, now let's get into the scripted greeting. Remember, this works based on the premise that you are executing every element we have discussed up to this point.

The perfect scripted greeting

1. "Welcome to our store have you been to our store before?"

The first words of the greeting are a question -- appropriately, because we need to take control right from the onset of the relationship and let the customer know that we are the expert and that we are in control. Whoever asks the questions is in control of the conversation. We are the experts in our store, and thus we need to be asking the questions. We are grooming the customer to be led by us.

Why is it so important to start with this question? The importance is not so much in the content as the intent. Asking a throwaway question like "How are you today?" is an invitation to the "I am just looking" response. Sure, asking how someone is today is technically a question, but one ever really means it to be more than a cursory greeting. They don't really want to hear anything other than "fine." When posed to a potential customer in a retail setting, it's a sure path to losing control of the conversation. Instead, be sincere and welcome a customer to your store as you would welcome a friend into your home, but be sure to go right into the rest of the question. Notice there is not a break or comma between, "Welcome to our store" and "have you been to our store before?" (You would put the name of your store in the script, i.e. "Welcome to Joe's Furniture".) This is because if you pause, the customer will fill in the dead space and start asking questions. An untrained salesperson would start answering those questions because they don't know any better. But we are trained salespeople and we are in charge! "Welcome to our store have you been here before?" forces the customer to deal with you, to make eye contact and address you as a human being and not just a salesperson.

Most of us grew up in America, with the vast majority of us going to public schools. In public school, we all learned basically the same way: we learned information, and when asked a question, we raced to raise our hands to answer first. We have been trained as a culture of reactors, of responders. When we know the answer, we don't think, we react.

While that is great for building a workforce, it's not that great for developing critical thinking skills. We are taking advantage of this lifelong training by asking our customer a question the moment we meet them, and they will feel obligated to answer. The important thing to remember is if we don't do this, they will ask the questions - - they will be in control. And while they will have the ability to ask questions, when they do it needs to be a conversation and not a question-and-answer session.

There is a local mattress chain in Northern California that is an interesting study when it comes to greeting customers. In their stores, they teach a technique called the "180 pass-by," which basically means as the customer walks in the store, you acknowledge them but then you quickly pass by them, acting busy. OK, I get why they do this, but what if I were to invite you over to my house, you'd walk in and instead of greeting you, I'd just buzz past you, say hi, and disappear into another room? Awkward, to say the least. What they are doing is acknowledging that customers are scared and apprehensive when they walk into their stores, and they react to this not by leading, but by mirroring the customer. The more effective action would be to first observe what the customer is observing when they walk in the door and then to identify the reasons they are feeling that way. Perhaps seeing balloons, hundreds of mattresses, bright lights and salespeople in ties is contributing to the already-heightened state of fear we discussed earlier.

If you have read anything about sales, or had any sales training, you are familiar with the term *mirroring*. Mirroring is taught in many seminars and books, and its basic premise is to make a customer feel more comfortable by imitating their body language. In my professional opinion, this is not an effective technique. If a customer is projecting bad posture or negative body language, you would not experience much success mirroring their already-negative body language. Instead of mirroring when you see negative body language, I would suggest a technique called *Observing and Influencing*. Observing and Influencing is the act of observing the customer's body language and adjusting your sales approach accordingly. For example, if the customer is standing with their arms folded, they are conveying that they are closed off. You would be ineffective mirroring such negative body language. Observing that they are closed-off is a sign that you need to get off the path you are on. This is also a great indication that you are talking too much or telling the customer something they don't believe or which they see as irrelevant. What you should do in this instance is stop talking and start asking the customer questions.

Ever try running down the street with your arms folded? It's awkward. You naturally want to unfurl your arms and let them swing side-to-side. Try this: try talking to a friend for a length of time with your arms folded. It's awkward. You will naturally want to use your hands to accentuate your words. Asking questions is a great way to get your customer talking and get them to open their arms and their minds. I have heard of some sales gurus who teach their trainees to offer the customer something, like a pen, to get them to open up their arms, but all this will accomplish is that your customer will have a pen in their hands and still won't believe a word you are saying.

Instead of mirroring, which is an action/reaction practice wherein you follow the customer's lead, the Observe/Influence technique teaches us to be the influence over the customer, and to set the example of the body language we want them to emulate. If you are smiling, open, expressive and confident, the customer will follow suit: they will open up and feel relaxed. If they feel threatened and nervous, you observe their reactions, get off the current course, use open and expressive body language and get them talking to build better rapport. If talking about the product or service is producing tension, get off the subject. Encourage the customer to talk about themselves, brag about their kids, etc.

Another advantage to asking if the customer has been to the store before is quite simple: if they have, we can find out if they have a relationship with someone else at the store. Many salespeople have other salespeople they work with, and some stores or companies pay based on individual salesperson performance. Qualifying a customer is a respectful practice, and if another salesperson already has a developed relationship with another customer, placing them back together will often help the company convert the customer into a sale. A typical exchange might sound like this:

Salesperson: "Welcome to Gem Furniture have you been to our store before?"
Customer: "Yes I have."
Salesperson: "Welcome back. Is there someone you have worked with in the past?"

This opens a window of opportunity for the customer to tell you if they are desirous of working with someone they have worked with before, or to reply that there is no one in particular they have worked with in your store before. I have seen salespeople subtly manipulate customers by changing the wording here, such as:

"Well, that person is busy, should I get them for you?"

Once a customer expresses an interest in returning to a salesperson they prefer, you should turn on your heels and get them that salesperson.

However, if you are by yourself or working in a different environment, once you have effectively and properly greeted the customer and they have answered your initial question, you can move forward with your greeting.

The body language that correlates with the first part of the greeting is vitally important to the success of the greeting. As previously discussed, incorrect body language and other factors can thwart your good intentions and start you off on a very bad footing with the customer.

First, give your customer time to get in the door and take in the environment. Let the door close behind them to avoid outside distractions. Next, be careful not to make the customer feel trapped against the door or in a corner. Always approach the customer slowly, deliberately and smoothly -- smiling, eyebrows up, head slightly tilted to the side and standing in a manner that allows the customer an escape. If you are squared up to the customer, they will feel like it's a stand-off, with no room to escape. By turning your body slightly, the customer can engage you or move if they are not comfortable. If the customer squares up to you, you can adjust to square up with them.

As you are approaching, you have your hands in an elevated, mid-torso high steeple. Then, as you begin with the first word of the greeting, open your hands to the customer, bringing them back together in a steeple as you conclude the first few words. Smile and ensure eye contact throughout the greeting.

Proximity is important when delivering the greeting as well. You want to avoid being too far from the customer when beginning the greeting, as the customer is less likely to hear you, and you are not going to develop as much intimacy with the customer from a distance. If the customer initiates things by saying hello from a distance, simply smile and approach, waiting until you have good eye contact and are at a comfortable talking distance. Then you may start your greeting.

2. "My name is Joe, what is your name?"

The second step in this greeting is the most powerful, and there are a lot of dynamics at work. We introduce ourselves, ask for the customer's name and offer our hand for a handshake.

First, let's discuss timing. The second line of the greeting is to be delivered immediately after the customer responds to the first part. You have their attention -- don't let them wiggle away. And if you pause after asking if they have been to the store before, the customer will often fill that dead air with questions, effectively taking control of the interaction and steering the sales potential of it. We are setting the foundation here for a relationship: one where we are going to lead the customer and establish that we have the solution for their problems and needs. Therefore it is imperative we establish from the beginning that this is our area of expertise, and we need to ask the questions to uncover the customer's issues so we can effectively solve them. If a customer begins peppering you with questions here, they could end up wresting control away from you with a bunch of questions that are not pertinent to solving their issue – this path often ends up with them asking you for your card or brochure. Walking out with your business card, they are left to try to marry the information you gave them with their problem.

For example, let's say you are expecting a new baby and you want to paint the baby's room a different color. You have learned enough about chemical exposure and off-gassing to know that you want to use a paint that does not emit harmful chemicals. So you go to the paint store looking to buy non-toxic paint. The first place you ask about non-toxic paint, the salesperson starts telling you about each and every one of the paints, their chemical makeup and formula, their drying times, etc. You start writing down all the information so you can make an informed decision, but it's a lot of information. You need to go home and think about it. All these different brands, different prices, they all do different things. Overwhelming.

So you go to the next paint store to comparison shop. But that salesperson recognizes that you don't want to become an expert in paint, you just want to paint your baby's room with non-toxic paint. He asks a few questions about the room, what you want to accomplish and what your concerns are, then using his technical knowledge, makes a couple of suggestions. Eureka! You buy the paint that's in your price range and does what you want it to do. The salesperson was smart enough to sell to your needs and wants, and not give you a bunch of information and let you discern if it would solve your problem and meet your needs.

"My name is Joe (you should insert your own name, ideally!), what is your name?"

Besides establishing that we are going to lead the customer, we also want to make them feel comfortable. At the beginning of the book we discussed the current state of retail and the misguided use of technology that further builds barriers between our store and the customer.

Customers are craving human interaction, not distance. They are starving for a sense of community and intimacy.

Chapter 5 Customer Intimacy

In the first chapter, I posed the question, "How many people have touched you today?" Unless you are married with kids jumping all over you in the morning, the likelihood that you go through your day without human touch is strong. Doctors tell us that we need four hugs per day to survive, eight hugs for maintenance and 12 hugs a day for growth. And yet we probably would have a hard time remembering the last time we even touched or were touched 12 times in a single day.

The fact is, as technology has become more advanced and a more dominant part of our lives, we have become more compartmentalized as a society and more dependent on technology as a means to profitability and efficient communication. Just because we have access to the amazing technology of computers and smartphones does not mean they are advantageous in every situation. Like we discussed earlier, these technological innovations have just given us more effective and efficient ways to alienate our customers and keep them at arm's length.

As more and more companies automate their operations, it leaves a major hole for other companies to fill and take advantage. Companies which recognize that their customers are human beings and that their companies consist of human beings can capitalize on this trend by re-humanizing their company's customer service and sales processes. At the sales level, it starts with touch, eye contact, a smile and a name. When we offer our name and reach out to the customer to shake their hand, we create an intimate bond with the customer -- we share their space.

Proximity

There is a comfortable space between you and a stranger. Proximity to another human being is such an interesting dynamic when you think about it. When attending a baseball game at the Oakland Coliseum, I walked into the men's room to find the traditional trough-type urinal, which meant I had to stand inches away from a total stranger in a very compromising position. It did not feel comfortable!

What does it feel like to have your space invaded? There is nervousness, fear and anxiety as a stranger gets too close. A great exercise I start off with when training all of my new staff is to have them stand in front of me. You can do this as well with a co-worker or if you can find a stranger brave enough. Now, I slowly step forward toward the person until we both feel that weirdness, that tension in the chest that makes us want to lean back away from the encroaching stranger. When you do it with a co-worker, you can perhaps get a bit closer, but there is a distinct barrier around you that sends an alarm when that space is violated.

Now, thinking back to all that fear and anxiety our customer has when they first walk into our store, just imagine how much extra anxiety it adds to the situation if we try to enter that forbidden space. So I take a step back from my trainee, but then I offer my hand in a traditional handshake gesture. Go ahead, try it -- shake their hand. Now, while shaking their hand, freeze. Notice something amazing? You are exactly at that same place that was intolerable before, but now you are perfectly comfortable. That weirdness and tension is non-existent. Why? A handshake is a social normalcy. It's universally accepted behavior, and thus, we don't feel that it is an intrusion. Just for fun, step back and then back into that space again without the handshake. Things become weird again!

What we do by offering our hand and shaking our customer's hand is powerful. We quickly narrow that "customer/salesman" chasm between us, having comfortably encroached on that forbidden zone -- which is vital if we are going to establish that we are a friend and not an enemy or a typical, self-interested salesperson. We have also touched, and in the touching we have established some intimacy with our customer. We may be the only person they touch all day, and that fact can be very influential in establishing a Retail Relationship with our customer. Also, in that touching the customer is forced to see us as a human being, not just a dispenser of information, someone in their way or someone who wants something from them.

Ever drive along the freeway at a crawl and some driver is trying to get over into your lane, in front of you? There is no reason for them to get over, and it's your spot. You keep your eyes focused straight ahead because it makes it simpler just to ignore the intruder. Once you look over, however -- once you make eye contact -- your resolve melts away and humanity takes over -- you let them in. The same principle is at work here. Once the customer makes eye contact with you, touches you, and you have stepped comfortably into their personal space, it is going to be much harder for the customer to run right over the top of you. They have to lower their guard. And we need them to lower their guard if we are going to lead them; if they are going to like us and buy from us. Remember, they will not buy from us if they don't like us. We have just a few moments for them to form an opinion of us, and in that first few moments, we can make a strong first impression and show them we are someone they should respect -- someone they need to deal with.

Here is another fun exercise: walk up to friends, family or colleagues and offer your hand in a handshake. Don't ask for it, and perhaps offer it at unusual times in the conversation. Watch how everyone reaches out to shake your hand in return. When you offer your hand to your customer it will be a very rare occasion when they don't return the gesture.

"Customers first buy us and then will buy anything we are selling. Conversely, if they don't buy you, you won't be able to sell them anything."

Another powerful thing happens in step two, and that is offering our name and asking the customer for their name. In that moment when you offer your hand for a handshake and give the customer your name, the customer will feel obligated to shake your hand and offer their name in return. This really starts to create a bond with the customer, and knowing the customer's name is another tool you can use to narrow the gap between you and the customer and get them to see you as a human being they can begin to like and trust.

Using the customer's name makes your customer, whose name you are calling out, feel warmly and positively towards you. People love to hear their name repeated back to them for the fact that it makes them stand out from a group of friends and other people. It makes them feel unique and special. Using a customer's name is also powerful because other salespeople do not use this technique and you are going to stand out, sound more personal and friendly, and be seen as a friend or as someone friendly; this means the customer will likely give you their business. If you have ever had to answer the phones at your business, or you have gotten marketing calls at home, you know that it is rather simple to hang up or say "no thanks" to a random telemarketer. But how much more difficult is it when they have your name? You feel more obliged to stay on the line, and you are less likely to hang up on them or be rude to them, because they know who you are! In our case, it would be much easier for the customer to avoid you or not buy from you if you never get them to lower their defenses, or never get them to see you as a human being. It's much easier to walk away if they don't have the makings of some relationship with you.

You are walking down the street and someone yells out your name from a passing car. You will stop instantly and look around. When someone says your name it is like an invisible leash, and people can get your attention by using it. The same dynamic happens when we have our customer's name and are diligent in using it throughout our conversation. Getting the name is important, but remembering and using it is the reason we are getting it in the first place.

There are lots of techniques for remembering your customer's name, but quite simply, do you forget your best friend's name? Of course not, because you have a relationship with them. You use their name all the time. I have a simple rule in my stores, called the *3-5 rule*. If you use the customer's name three to five times in the first few moments of the greeting, you will have no trouble remembering it. And if they have a hard-to-pronounce name, even better! The customer is well aware that their name is hard-to-pronounce and are used to people struggling with it. It is perfectly acceptable to repeat it back to them slowly upon meeting them, to ensure you have it correctly. Now it will be easy to understand and remember because you have repeated it a couple of times. There is no greater offense in my stores than a salesperson spending an hour with a customer, speaking about their issues, their kids and their lives, only to have to ask their name again at the register. Unspeakable! If you do forget the name, it is better to apologize on the sales floor and ask for it again, then continue using it. However, if you use the 3-5 rule, you will rarely, if ever, have this issue.

What are some of the common mistakes made by salespeople in the above steps?

The first and most common mistake is approaching the customer at the beginning too aggressively. The other day while I was training a new salesperson on these techniques, and on cue a customer came into the store with their dog -- and was it ever a skittish and nippy dog! I could not believe it – it was like a poorly-written movie. We had just discussed the scared dog and the friendly dog scenario when approaching customers, and here we had a scared dog on a leash in our store! Needless to say I could not resist the temptation to illustrate the technique.

This dog was very nervous and barked at the slightest movement. When I tried to approach the dog, it shied behind its owner and bared its teeth. Then I got on my hands and knees and offered my hand, palms up, very slowly, and the dog came out from behind the owner sniffed my hand. I got up, approached tall again, the dog cowered. I got down low, moved slowly, and the dog responded. Classic.

Time and time again I have seen this technique not work and the salesperson blames the technique, never recognizing that they approached too aggressively. In all my years of employing this technique, I personally have rarely had issue with it because first of all, I read the person coming through the door. If they are reserved and standoff-ish, I slow down, talk softly, tilt my head and offer my hand slowly. If they are outgoing and engaging, it works just fine to approach them normally.

Another issue I have seen is when a salesperson does not give the customer time to get in the door and the customer never has a moment to adjust to their new surroundings. The noise from the outside is still in their ears and they have no idea what the salesperson has just said. Give the customer a moment to get in the door, let the door close, and let the customer make eye contact with you, *Then* start your greeting. The customer should be able to see you when you are speaking. Also, along these lines, I have seen salespeople start the greeting when the customer is looking away from them, not wanting to make that initial eye contact. Big mistake. If you want to be heard and valued, get the customer to look at you first. You can do this by saying that first "Welcome" a bit louder, then going back to a normal or softer tone. This will usually get the customer's attention.

Sometimes you will have customers who won't want to shake your hand for religious or sanitary reasons. No worries: just keep smiling and execute the rest of your greeting. Getting their name and using it, building rapport and using proper body language will help you develop your Retail Relationship, even in the absence of a physical handshake. The same thing might happen when you ask for your customer's name and they fail for whatever reason to give it. Remember, these techniques are very powerful and will result in more sales, so don't worry or concern yourself with the .001% of customers who don't respond to you. Just smile and do everything else the right way.

3. "Mike and Sally, nice to meet you. How did you hear about our store?"

Of course, once you have the customer's name, use it right away, like we have discussed. And the perfect place to use it is at the start of the next question. Addressing the customer by name, making eye contact, displaying proper body language (steepling and open-palm gestures), and asking them how they heard about your store. Three questions in a row:

"Have you been here before?"

"What is your name?" and

"How did you hear about us?"

Let the customer know that you are in control of the interaction and that you have a plan -- that you are leading. Another thing is occurring: you are getting answers. Your customer is talking. And if you are smart, you are listening.

People love to talk about themselves. To someone who may experience precious few human interactions over the course of their day, a conversation can be tremendously desirable and satisfying. Next to a love of talking about themselves, people really love and value someone who listens to them. Someone who *really* listens -- not just waits for them to finish talking so they can butt right back in and resume the monologue. And if you *really* listen to the answers to the questions you ask, your customer will tell you everything you need to know about how to sell to them.

Most sales books I have read and companies I have worked for stressed building a presentation. A presentation is comprised of us talking, with the customer listening. A more effective way of selling is to ditch the presentation, get your customer talking and have a conversation; one where the customer shares their concerns and you address their concerns, and then the customer affirms that they can see how the product you have on offer will solve their concerns.

"And if you really listen to the answers to the

questions you ask,

your customer will tell you everything you

need to know about how to sell to them."

Growing up, I loved to read "Sherlock Holmes" mystery novels. Sherlock Holmes was a master at observation and gathering evidence no one else would notice. He could tell in what part of town you lived by the crumb on your lapel or the mud on your shoe. A well-trained salesperson understands that the most effective tool they have in sales is a properly-formed question and the information the subsequent answer provides, as you build the momentum and index of knowledge of the customer that unlocks the sale.

When you ask a question, customers will open up and start talking. So the simple question of "How did you hear about us?" can yield lots of clues about the customer's motivation for coming to the store and what their wants and needs are. The more your customer opens up to you, the more they are going to let their guard down and the more they let their guard down, the more they will like you, trust you, and ultimately buy from you. You are well on your way to developing the perfect Retail Relationship.

In review, what have we learned?

We make eye contact with the customer, we smile, we welcome the customer actively and we initiate contact with the customer -- we take the lead. And if we don't, the customer will. And rarely will they lead you to the cash register.

We offer our name, get the customer's name and use it. This helps us jump-start the process of building intimacy and trust with our customer. Without trust, you have no sale, and customers are not able to let their guard down. Customers ultimately want to be listened to and valued, because like all human beings they like the attention and the social interaction.

We ask them how they heard about us. It helps us start to uncover clues about what motivated them to come to our store, about what they want and need, and ultimately we will discover how this will help us sell to them.

Many things happen in this short amount of time upon greeting the customer: We get the customer's name and use it often, helping them develop trust and lowering their defenses. We touch them in appropriate, rapport-building ways, helping build intimacy and trust. We ask a series of questions, preparing them for the sales process, in which we are going to have a conversation and we being the expert, we are going to diagnose their issues -- not just wait for them to fire off a bunch of questions. And all the while we are smiling, relaxed and conveying body language that is strong and confident. This is the foundation for leading the customer to a perfect sale and a great Retail Relationship.

Where to now?

You have the customer's full attention and have intimated to the customer that you are going to lead, so where to now? No matter what you are selling -- no matter what product you are representing – if you are going to lead the customer where you both want to go, you have to understand the customer's problems, needs and wants as they relate to the product you are trying to sell them.

I am reminded of the story of an Omaha Steaks salesman who was very good at getting people to buy beef. One day he knocked on the door of a woman, introduced himself and started to give her his pitch, about how Omaha Steaks are the finest steaks on the planet. That the cows are fed natural, lush, green grasses high on the Montana plains, far from pollution and chemical fertilizers. That they are raised cruelty-free, and never given growth hormones or antibiotics.

And the steaks! He went into lush detail about the meat's most amazingly luscious aroma, and how the steaks melt in your mouth like the proverbial butter. He asserted that he would bet that they are the best steaks she would ever buy – and if he was wrong, he'd be glad to give her twice her money back. The salesman couldn't have been prouder of his pitch.

The woman nonchalantly stated she was a vegetarian and shut the door.

What did he miss? A simple question -- simply taking a few moments to get to know his customer as a human being and understanding her wants and needs could have led him to ask if she liked to eat steak. Had she said no, he could have asked if she knew anyone who did. If she said her father did, he could have customized his entire pitch around why Omaha Steaks make a great gift.

Earlier in this book I stated that whoever is asking the questions is in control of the conversation. And listening to the responses to those questions will help you understand how and what to sell to your customer. Now, get ready to learn a very powerful technique called *The Objectionless Close*.

Chapter 6 The Objectionless Close

In our mattress stores we sell thousands of mattresses a year, yet we have never once asked for the sale. Anyone in sales knows you have to ask for a sale, right? There are countless books devoted to nothing but how to close a sale and to closing techniques. There are hundreds of closing tricks, some with fancy and exotic names -- techniques designed to get your customer to buy. When I tell people that we never ask for a sale in our stores, they are not sure how to process this information. We don't ask how they are going to pay for it, we don't tell them it's going off sale at the end of the day, we don't tell them they get a special deal if they buy two of them. We simply lead them to the solution. The customer tells us they want to buy and we ring them up.

The Objectionless Close technique was created in an interesting environment: a dating company. I was hired by a company called Table For Six to run their sales department. They had three locations at the time, with a sales staff of three ladies in each location. The company gave singles events and dinners at which their clients could meet and mingle with other single adults.

The service was very expensive, and the sales process was one of intense pressure. The prospective clients would email to declare their interest, and the sales staff -- or "counselors" -- would contact the prospective clients and coax them to come in for an appointment to learn about the service. They were not allowed to discuss pricing over the phone, which made it difficult to get people to reliably show up for appointments. But once the prospective client came in, the counselor would sit them down and start the interview process.

The interview process would last an hour or two as the counselor and prospective client would chat back and forth, with the counselor asking a series of questions. Then, at the end, the counselor would break out a binder with photos of happy couples and the pricing. Ouch! Four grand to go out on dinners and events? That you had to pay for on top of the fee to join?! Needless to say, they were not experiencing high closing rates.

After breaking down the process, I came up with the Objectionless Close. My plan was simple: I had the ladies write down every possible objection they had ever heard, and any others they could think of additionally. Then, I had them come up with a corresponding answer to that objection. Then, I changed their thinking: It was only an objection if once they asked for the sale, the customer raised the concern. But if they unearthed the concern *before* the close, it was just a topic of conversation.

They saw the light at the end of their tunnel! There is no resistance to what you are selling if you address every concern during the conversation phase of the sale. If you try to force the sale closed while leaving concerns lingering, those concerns inevitably turn into nearly insurmountable objections. I call it "climbing the waterfall": near impossible and the most slippery of slopes imaginable. Once the customer has told you no, any good will you had built up in the conversation phase has been eradicated and replaced with bad feelings. No one likes to be pushed and manipulated.

The first time the counselors at the dating company tried out their new sales tools they were extremely successful, and we saw revenue shoot through the roof. So much so that the former owner of the business called me up and took me to task for making more money than she did that first month.

The number one objection the counselors would face, of course, was that the service was too expensive. To solve this problem, during the conversation phase of the sale, our counselor asked the prospective client if they were opposed to spending money on themselves. They would ask what their last major purchase was, and then had the customer reiterate they had no problem making a major purchase if something made them happy and if it was something that they really wanted. Then, of course, the logical next step was to use questions and visualization to get the prospective client to tell our counselor just how important it was to find a mate -- how it would change their life, and how it would be more valuable than anything they could otherwise purchase. How would the prospective client then say no at the conclusion of the sale? The vast majority of the time they swallowed hard at seeing the price, but through using questions, they had talked themselves right into a membership. And thus was born the Objectionless Close. If you can bring up in conversation every possible objection and concern, uncover the true reason for the concern -- and once uncovered, discuss and solve that problem -- at the end of the sale, the customer talks themselves into the purchase. It's the logical conclusion. Now you can start to see why we never have to ask for a sale in our stores.

The Objectionless Close begins in those first few moments, when the customer is forming their opinion of us. It continues with us sticking to our greeting script and executing it perfectly -- leading the customer, asking questions and listening. The next step in this process is yet another technique you need to master. It's more of a formula actually, and understanding and applying it to your sales process -- along with a few other techniques I will teach you -- will lead you seamlessly to an Objectionless Close.

The formula you need to learn and identify is simply $U+D=M$, which is short for

Urgency + Desire = Motion

U+D=M is the universal process behind all sales decisions. When this formula is applied to your sales tools -- when you learn to recognize, uncover and apply this formula to your customers -- you will unlock one of the primary powers of the Objectionless Close.

What is U+D=M?

Urgency means a force or impulse that impels or constrains. For example, when you feel hunger pains, you are moved to feed that hunger. When you see a punch coming at you, you feel an overwhelming and insistent urgency to move out of harm's way or to defend yourself. Urgency is a feeling that motivates motion and action.

Desire is deep longing or want. It is the state of wanting something and being convinced you must have it. When you desire someone, you will do the craziest things to get next to that person. When you desire an object, you will save, steal, and strive to achieve or acquire it by whatever means available to you.

When you have urgency and desire, you have motion. For example, let's say you just moved to a new house and you have no mattress. Sleeping on the floor is uncomfortable, and because you don't have a mattress, you now have an urgency – via an immediate and compelling reason -- to get a mattress. Discomfort and lack of sleep because of the absence of a viable mattress has created an urgency. If you had a couch to sleep on that was somewhat comfortable, perhaps that would diminish the urgency, but having nowhere to sleep but a cold, hard floor leads to urgency. That urgency drives you out into the retail environment, where you start looking for a mattress. You enter one store only to find their mattresses are too firm. You have plenty of urgency, but you don't desire any of their selection of mattresses. You go to the next store and find their mattresses comfortable and in your price range. You desire their mattresses. Urgency plus Desire equals Motion: in this case the motion of buying a mattress.

Without these two essential elements, you will not get the desired outcome of a sale. Someone might love your mattress selection, but they are not moving to the area for six months yet. Desire but no urgency. Companies have been creating false urgency for as long as people have sold to other people. It's called a sale. A sale creates a motivator -- an urgency -- to buy at that time. But false urgency often leads to feelings of anger and mistrust with customers, who find themselves disliking being forced into buying something until they are truly ready. False urgency sometimes works temporarily, but it wears off and is therefore not the most powerful selling tool. The most powerful urgency is the customer's own, legitimately felt urgency.

Desire is also something you can falsify to an extent. Companies spend billions making their product seem sexy, and hiring models and actresses to endorse or use their product, thus creating a manufactured sense of desire in the marketplace. But again, desire born out of the customer's own feelings and wants – and not handed to them wholesale from someone or somewhere else -- is the most powerful.

Discovering your customers' urgency and desire is a requirement in building the Objectionless Close. Once you discover the urgency and desire -- once you get the customers to admit and confess their urgency and desire -- you can sell to that urgency and desire. How do we uncover the customer's urgency and desire?

Find the pain, poke the pain, alleviate the pain

Once you have your customer's trust and gotten past their defenses, it's time to start asking questions to determine what it is that your customer really wants. For the sake of example, I will use our mattress store and what we do.

The basic premise that we adhere to is that no one goes to McDonald's to look at the menu. They go there to eat because they are hungry, and everyone knows what they have. The employees behind the counter don't have to try to sell you food, they simply say, "How can I take your order?" We adhere to the same belief in our mattress stores: that customers don't come to a mattress store unless, in their minds, they need a mattress. So there is already an understanding on our part. Our challenge is to get the customer to confess to us their urgency -- their need -- so we can lead them to the solution to that urgency.

No one likes to admit they are lost. It's a feeling of vulnerability that invokes fear and confusion. When customers have a need and they are searching for a solution, there is often a feeling of vulnerability. Only when the customer feels they can trust someone will they open up and confess their need. And only when they confess their need can we address their need.

When we are working with customers in the mattress store, we are immediately seeking clues from the customer by utilizing questions, to discover their urgency and desire. After we conduct our greeting, we ask the customer to tell us what they are sleeping on currently. This is a very effective tool as it starts to get the customer thinking about the reason they were spurred into the store. Once they are thinking about it, they are thinking about the pain -- the discomfort --

associated with what they are currently sleeping on, or not sleeping on. That is the pain, and once we have identified that pain we need to provoke their perception of it in the moment, so the customer's pain will become real – that is, actionable upon in terms of solutions -- and in the forefront of their mind as they consider the solution to that pain.

Visualization is a powerful tool to use in this process. Ever been to a scary movie? Did you flinch or scream at a really scary part? How about a sad movie? Did you feel like crying? Why? It's not real, it's just a fabric screen onto which are projected make-believe images. There is no real pain or danger. Yet there is a strong force at work: the imagination. At the movies, the mind is not capable of discerning make-believe from reality. It takes in the images and reacts as if they were real, as the suspension of disbelief required for entertainment is produced. Heavy stuff! We are going to take advantage of this dynamic by asking the customer to tell us about their current mattress, and in doing so, they are going to visualize their lumpy old caved-in mattress that is killing their back night after night and they are going to feel that pain all over again. Find the pain, provoke its perception.

Back to when I ran the sales staff of the high-end dating service: It was surely one of the hardest types of sales I have ever had to make. Prospects had to be enticed to come in with a minimum of information and no idea of the cost. Once seated, the salesperson had to interview them and get them to plop down $4,000.00 for the service. Visualization played a big part in our sales presentation. Because we were dealing with an emotion-based service, evoking pain and alleviating it was an important part of the presentation. If the prospect did not feel desperate enough to meet someone, they would not see the value of the service.

I supervised every presentation by listening in on the conversation between my staff and the prospect. This particular day, my new salesperson, Yolanda, was interviewing a woman in her late forties who wanted to get married. During the interview process, the prospect told Yolanda about a trip to a foreign country she had planned. Yolanda excitedly leaned across the table and proclaimed

"Wouldn't it be amazing to have someone to go on that trip with you?"

Now, I can see why she thought this was a good idea. Sure, perhaps the woman would have loved someone to go with her. However, she missed a golden opportunity to ask the prospect to visualize the possibilities. How much more effective would it had been if Yolanda had asked

"What would it be like to have someone to go with you?"
Then the prospect would immediately picture that and feel the emotions of the picture in her mind. Instead of being told it was amazing, she could imagine it and feel what it might be like in her own context and on her own, uniquely personal terms. Also, what Yolanda assumed is that she wanted someone to go with her. Perhaps the trip was a pilgrimage the prospect needed to make alone. By inserting someone into her imagination of the trip, she could have offended the prospect and pushed her away, leaving her feeling inappropriately intruded upon. But by asking the prospect how it would feel to put the power in her own hands and head -- allowing

her to fill in the gaps or reject the idea -- allowed Yolanda to merely ask a question. Visualization is much more powerful when we ask the customer to come up with a picture in their mind than it is to force one on them and risk the picture not being one that is welcome.

Now that we have found and provoked the perception of the pain, during the conversation about our products and the customer's issues, we will be executing another technique called *Drilling Down*. Drilling Down is a technique designed to understand the deeper issue presented by the customer, or to discover the true intent behind a question. We will get more into the question aspect, but for now, drilling down into the pain brings urgency to the top of the customer's mind. It's certainly a more powerful motivator than creating false urgency, and the customer feels that they are choosing the solution because we are not forcing one on them.

For example, telling the customer that they can get a great deal -- but that it's only for today -- creates not urgency, but animosity. The customer now feels pushed and cajoled into making a decision. But when you *drill down* into the pain, asking the customer to describe their current mattress to tell you how it is affecting their life, their sleep, and their health, the customer revisits all the painful reasons they are there and reaffirms to them that they need a new mattress. They choose; you don't push. When you utilize this technique, you maintain the trust, good feelings and friendship you have developed with the customer. The minute you push, you are no longer a trusted consultant or friend; you are just another salesperson -- the enemy.

Alleviate the Pain

Once you have clearly identified the pain and effectively asked your customer to relive the pain, you now need to alleviate the pain. Knowing your customer's needs is what makes it very simple to sell them. You would think this is obvious, but it is amazing to me how many salespeople I have met in my life who are convinced they have the perfect pitch memorized and can't wait to impress you with how much they know about a product, with little or no attention paid or sensitivity developed to the needs and wants that have driven the customer to enter the store in the first place.

Which of these two scenarios do you think is more effective? You sit down at a restaurant and the waiter starts to list off a bunch of ingredients, leaving you to consider all these elements, the amount of them used, and then to imagine what the dish would be or how it would taste.. Or, you sit down and the waiter comes over and paints a word picture describing a succulent meal, illustrating in vivid detail the tastes and smells. A good waiter can describe a dish and make your mouth water.

The competitor I spoke of earlier in the book -- the mattress store in Northern California -- prides itself on taking six weeks to train their staff. Six weeks! To sell a mattress! Let me tell you a secret: A mattress is comprised of layers of foam and fibers on top of a base of springs or a foam base. That's it. Oh, there is one company that uses an air mattress for the base. And once you have the construction down, there are but three types: firm, medium and soft. Congratulations, you just became a mattress expert.

But somehow, this mattress chain is able to squeeze all that into about four weeks of training, and another two weeks teaching general sales skills. So, here we have four weeks of technical training, with all these facts and details such as coil counts, foam densities, heat-tempered coils, etc., stuffed into the heads of the salespeople and they cannot wait for you to ask a question so they can deluge you with all this information and dazzle you with facts.

However, the problem with this type of selling, like the earlier example of the waiter giving you the ingredients instead of the description of the dish, is that you have to trust the customer will ask all the right questions to solve their own problems. Guess what? They usually get overwhelmed and leave, stating they need to think about it, and they do, because they are more confused than when they first came in.

The customer does not want to become a mattress expert, they just want to solve their problem and get on with a life enriched by the product you are selling. All that technical information is good for one thing: for you to ask questions, uncover the customer's urgency and desire, and then apply your knowledge to their issues to solve them. Alleviate their pain.

More on Drilling Down

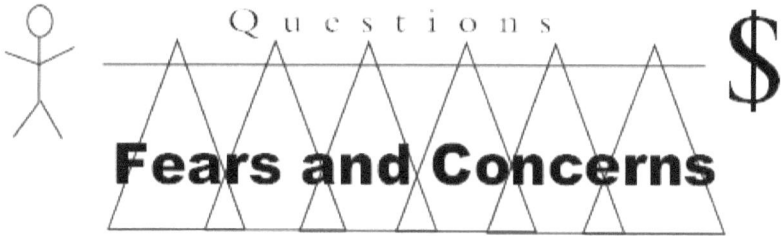

Once you get the laughter out of your system caused by the sophistication of my illustration, let's look at what is represented here. Your customer is represented by the stick figure on the left, and the sale is on the right. In between is a line that represents the sales conversation. Please note that I call it a sales conversation and not a presentation. A presentation is typically where you talk and the customer listens. A proper sale is you talking about 30-40% of the time, with the customer talking about 60-70% of the time. That is called a conversation, one where you are asking questions; your customer is giving you information and expressing to you their issues, and you are explaining why and how your product will solve those issues.

The triangles are the fears and concerns the customer has and they manifest into the conversation as questions. Customers ask questions out of fear and concern. Fear is a great force in our lives, and fear is capable of derailing any sale if it is left unaddressed. Fears often pop up in the guise of innocent questions. A very well-trained salesperson is listening intently and watching for these roadblocks between them and the sale.

See those little peaks poking up into the conversation? Those are the roadblocks that, if not answered, will prevent you from getting the sale. It is very common for the salesperson to correctly answer every question and not get the sale because they did not take the time to dig down into each question and address the underlying fear and concern.

For example, let's say that when the customer was last shopping for a mattress, they asked the salesperson if the mattress would last a long time. The salesperson confidently assured them the mattress was well-made and would last 10 years. Five years later they come to your store, their back killing them because the mattress did not hold up. When they ask you if the mattress will hold up over a long life, you tell them it is well-made and will last 10 years. Guess what? You are not going to have much success and the customer will likely leave with a business card. Why? Because you did not stop and think, stop and drill down, uncovering the fear and concern underneath the question about the length of the life of the mattress, which was one of the central driving forces behind the customer's concern about your product.

Earlier in the book we were talking about how people are trained to react when they know an answer: they enthusiastically regurgitate learned information. It is not just customers who do this, it is salespeople as well. Remember the six weeks of training I spoke of the other guys receiving? They have been trained to respond with the correct information when asked a certain question. However, I want to teach you a technique that will set you apart from all the other salespeople and give you the edge over these kinds of sales robots.

Real customer review

Before I even walked in the door, Joe came over to welcome me into the store, and was genuinely warm and friendly. The store is small and super inviting -- clean, and not overwhelming. Joe answered all my questions about the two lines of beds that he offers, and gave me all the time and space I needed to lay on them and test them out. He never once pressured me into a sale, or try to "lock the price down" as some of the big box stores did to me. No cheesy sales tactics here -- just solid, honest, easy to verify information.

When someone asks you a question, you need to train your brain to create some space between the question and the answer. Instead of reacting to the question and answering it immediately because you know the answer, I want you to use that space you create to think.

I know that we weren't trained in school to think, we were trained to react. But I need you to think. Think about the *why* of the question your customer is asking. What is the concern -- the fear -- driving this question to the forefront of their mind? The picture plays out in the customer's head something like this when there are fears: "I want to buy this… *but*." The "but" is what will prevent them from arriving at the realization the product will solve their issues and stops them from ultimately making the purchase. If you can address and remove the "but," the customer will come to the logical conclusion that the product will solve their issue, and they will choose the product. If you have effectively found, provoked and alleviated the pain, the customer will arrive at the decision on their own. Not because you pushed, but because you helped them convince themselves.

Pain is a great motivator. And the relief of pain is an emotional drug. When you discover the pain and provoke the pain, the customer remembers what it is like to feel the pain that drove them to seek out your product; the customer revisits and feels the pain. When you alleviate it for the customer, they feel the relief of the pain emotionally, just like when we talked about being at the movies and feeling the sadness of a sad movie or the fear generated by a horror film. That relief is real, and you are suddenly the customer's hero.

When you effectively drill down, listen to the customer's questions, explore and discover the motivating factor behind those questions, and address the questions *and* the pain, only then will you completely clear the path to the sale.

When customers come into our store, one of the common questions they ask is whether our mattress will retain a body impression. What customers are really saying is their last mattress did not last, and how can they trust that yours will? Our staff is trained to ask if they had an issue with their last mattress retaining a body impression. If the customer says yes, we are careful not only to explain why their last mattress retained an impression and why ours won't, but to assure them that if they did not want a body impression again, our mattress would be the one to buy. And we tie the whole exchange off with a perfect ribbon bow (absolutely no balloons, though) by following our answer up with a question of our own so we can continue to lead the conversation.

Another question we get a lot, thanks to the way our competitors do business, is "What kind of a deal can you make me?" or, "Is this your best price?" Our well-trained staff recognizes where this question emanates from: either the customer is not trusting us or they are afraid to buy and find out down the road it's going to go on sale and someone else will have benefited from a better price. By drilling down and addressing the concern instead of the question, we are able to avoid bargaining with the customer without making them feel bad for not getting a better deal.

Drilling down and discovering the urgency and desire -- and selling to that urgency and desire -- are two of the major components of performing an Objectionless Close. Using these techniques, our sales staff is able to sell mattresses every day and build friendships with our customers, all the while without having to ask for the sale. We don't push, we lead. And the customer follows, and buys.

"Let me ask you a question..."

Learn this phrase because it is a salesperson's best friend. Customers have the best intentions at heart when they ask questions: they just want to know the answer to their concern. However, customers are not the experts, you are. You are very well-educated and experienced when it comes to your product or service. The customer has concerns. We want them to express concerns, and we encourage them to ask questions, but in the context of a conversation if we let the customer lead the conversation we run the risk of the customer not asking the correct questions to address all of their issues, all of their fears and all of their concerns.

Questions are good. They give us clues to the customer's concerns and fears, but we need it to be a conversation and not a situation where they ask all the questions and we just answer all the questions. It is very frustrating when I observe one of my salespeople get led around the sales floor by a customer. The customer asks a question, the salesperson answers and then stands there waiting for the next question. The customer then feels obligated to fill the dead air with another question, another question and another question. This usually results in the customer ultimately asking for a brochure, as they need to go home and try to make sense of all the specs and information the salesperson regurgitated in lieu of leading the customer to the sale.

The other day, we had a customer come into the store: a man who, you could tell, was used to being in charge. My newest salesperson was still a bit green with his greeting, so when he approached the customer a bit timidly, the customer almost ran right over the top of him like a 16-wheeler. When my salesperson welcomed him to the store and asked if he had been there before, the customer disregarded the question and just went right into asking the salesperson a question: "Tell me about your mattresses."

Remembering his training, he responded to the question perfectly: "We make a durable, comfortable, affordable mattress, but let me ask you a question. How did you hear about us?" Beautifully executed save! The customer was ready to just run over the top of the salesperson and lead the conversation. But my salesperson was able to use that simple phrase to steer the conversation back to the direction he needed and get the customer's attention so he could make a perfect sale and begin a stellar Retail Relationship.

I used to work at a mattress store in Oahu, Hawai'i, and since it is a relatively small place, I was familiar with all the other mattress stores on the island. So when customers would come into the store with the business card of a salesperson at another mattress store, I knew it would be an easy sale because I knew what they had seen and experienced. When I greeted them, the customers would have a lost look, displaying body language which showed they were confused and needing direction. These customers would have a business card from the other mattress store's salesperson, and they would read off the information the salesperson had written on the back of the card. After I greeted them, they would ask, "Do you have such and such mattress with this many coils, etc.?" Poor customers! They had run into a salesperson who gave them a bunch of facts and specs and these customers didn't have a clue how any of the information on the back of that business card was going to result in a solution to their issues. I would take the card and instead of answering the question, I would ask one of my own:

"Why is any of this information important?"

The customer was taken aback. They didn't know that answer.

When you can get your customer to admit they are lost, gently exposing their need for help, and you have shown them you are confident, trustworthy and genuinely care about them, they will turn over the reins of the sale and buy what you suggest. The minute you hear or sense the customer in that "Um" moment -- that moment they realize they need to be led -- you need to confidently step in and take the control they are offering you and show them that you have confidence that you can solve their issues.

Back to the group of salespeople at the Hispanic Yellow Pages I discussed earlier in the book. After observing them in the field and helping them see that the common ground between salespeople and customers is that each are human beings -- and that they needed to communicate from that premise -- I gave them a technique which gave them control of the sales process and a renewed sense of confidence.

They were used to going into a sales conversation and, having identified the decision-maker among whomever it was they were selling to, they would do what most salespeople do: make a presentation. And their presentation was often met with, "I'm not interested." What I taught them is that they first needed to get the decision-maker to admit their need. They could accomplish this by asking one simple question: "How are you currently reaching the Hispanic market?" The decision-maker would almost always pause and say "Um." And the moment you get an "Um" they admit they are lost, and you are now the expert. You then can provoke the perception of that pain – the feeling of absence and loss and bases left uncovered -- and take advantage of the decision-maker being uninformed. "Did you know that in this market, over 40% of the population is Spanish speaking? How would it affect your business to have a 40% increase?" Once the decision-maker admits their need, now the salesperson can sell to that need.

I could see smiles all across the room when I taught them this technique. There was a palpable excitement in the room as the salespeople could see this as their path to a resistance-free sale.

They saw a path they did not see before and were ready to get out in the market and try their new sales tool.

When you get the customer to admit their pain, their urgency, and their need, they are open to being led to a solution by someone they trust. And if you have followed all the steps properly, the person they trust will be you.

Not every question, however, should be about the sale. In building a Retail Relationship, you want to build rapport and we again use questions to do this.

Rapport Building: Its importance and the *when* and *why*

I received a nice email last night from a customer I assisted several months ago. They sent me a photo of their newborn baby. When they had come into the store, we talked about their life, their move, their new place, their first baby on the way and their love of surfing. Several months after the sale, the customer felt a connection still --

enough to send me a photo of their baby and the proud parents -- and invited me to go out surfing with them sometime.

Many years ago, before the internet's prevalence, companies would hire "Secret Shoppers" to come into their stores to pose as shoppers and evaluate the store's sales staff and their performance. With review sites such as Yelp.com now having such an influence in the marketplace, Secret Shoppers are not as important as they once were. Review sites encourage customers to post their experience with a product and the store they purchased from, giving the world a place to read recommendations, but more importantly giving stores the ability to read unbiased opinions of their service. I was having a conversation the other day with a fellow retailer who made a powerful statement: "If you have a store in San Francisco and you have bad Yelp reviews, you might as well close up shop and start over." Review sites are changing the way we do business, and smart salespeople are taking advantage of this powerful marketing tool.

Review sites are one of the tools I use to gauge how successful our store staff is and how our company policies affecting customers are received. If I see a complaint, I can quickly identify a possible procedure or policy that may need tweaking. One of the most powerful testimonies to our staff and our sales techniques is the prevalence of reviews from customers noting our sales staff's names.

Think about your last retail purchase: Do you recall the salesperson's name? Likely you do not, unless it was a really big purchase and they did either a memorably great job or a very poor job. The overwhelming majority of our reviews are written by customers who are proud to identify to others, by name, the salesperson who took their time with them, was patient -- not pushy -- and who listened to them and helped them make an informed purchase. In fact, as I was typing out this paragraph, I had an email notification pop up, announcing a new review on Yelp. I opened it to find yet another 5-star review, with my salesperson being thanked by name. This tells me my team is following their training and taking the lead, building in the process a relationship with the customer. One of the tools we use in our stores is rapport building.

Real customer review

After dealing with other mattress vendors around the area, including the big chains and some local dealers, there was something about Nest that brought us back. The staff that we dealt with, both Joe and the rest of the staff, were both helpful and knowledgeable. The explanation of where natural materials mattered and where they didn't was forthright. The lack of high-pressure sales was a huge bonus. Would absolutely recommend again.

Personally, when selling, I don't talk about specs and facts much. The majority of the conversation I have with my customers has always been primarily about themselves, about their lives, what they do for a living, their passions and their lifestyle. During these conversations we discover commonalities and we talk about shared interests and passions.

Somewhere in the middle of these conversations, the customer decides that they find my company enjoyable, and they like and appreciate the fact I am really listening to them and showing an interest in their lives. It's sincere too, because I genuinely do find people interesting and a salesperson who tries to fake that interest gets exposed and avoided like the Plague.

In the midst of rapport building the customer has told me everything I need to know about how to sell them, about what they want and need -- their desires -- and will give me their business, whether it's during that particular visit to the store or a return visit. If they feel the need to go elsewhere to shop and assuage their curiosity or fear they may be missing out on a better deal, but they almost always come back because no one else took the time to get to know them. People want to feel they are buying from a friend.

The first step in building rapport is having the intent to build rapport. You have to genuinely want to take the time and effort to build a relationship with your customer. I like to remind my staff they are onstage, like an actor or actress in a play. When customers come into the store, they are onstage to perform for the customer. The customer does not want to hear about the salesperson's bad day or problems at home. They want to be entertained, enlightened, and they want *their* problems solved, not to be burdened with our issue but to be set free and have their needs met by our best selves. So it is important to ensure each day you put your personal issues aside and focus on the customer and your job. You simply must focus on making a fun, informative and entertaining retail experience for the customer.

Following the steps I have outlined for a proper sale will build the foundation for rapport. You leading confidently, with the touch of a handshake and a diminishing of the proximity between you and the customer, getting their name and using their name, asking questions and drilling down -- all of these techniques encourage the customer to relax and open up to you.

Once you have properly established the foundation for rapport, be sure to begin asking the customer some more personal questions about themselves. Nothing too personal at the onset -- stick to questions which are more socially acceptable, such as where they live, what they do, etc. As the conversation progresses you can ask deeper, more probing questions. Asking questions which are too personal too soon can destroy all of the good feelings you have worked hard to establish.

I had a set of customers come into my store one day, a man and woman. After greeting them and leading them, I began asking some questions specific to their situation. Because of the disparity in age between the man and woman, I was having a difficult time discerning if they were a couple or a father and daughter. Since the man was doing the talking, I asked him if he slept alone or if he slept with a partner. The customer became deeply offended and stomped out of the store. I had gotten a bit ahead of myself and had not built enough rapport to ask the question as bluntly as I did, and lost a customer. Had I taken a bit more time to get to know the customer and watch for body language clues, I could have discovered the information I needed to sell to their needs.

Another great tool in rapport-building is the classic *Feel, Felt, Found* technique. This technique is designed to keep you from being at odds with the customer when they make a challenge statement. For example, when a customer comes into our store and makes the statement, "I don't like memory foam," our staff does not challenge the statement but rather agrees that many customers feel the same way -- but once they've felt our foam, they found it to be quite different.

The common mistake salespeople make when a customer makes a challenge statement is to take the defensive posture and ask the customer what they don't like about the subject matter. For instance, with the above example, a common response would be, "What don't you like about memory foam?" A challenge statement is a line drawn in the sand, with the customer stating a deeply-held conviction. The least effective thing to do would be to become defensive, asking the customer to reinforce their deeply-held conviction by restating their convictions and then trying to convince them otherwise. This attempt at convincing is nothing more than telling the customer their deeply-held conviction is wrong. And doing so will kill or deeply injure any rapport you have built or hope to build.

The most effective way to handle a challenge statement is to step over that line drawn in the sand by the customer, figuratively put your hand around their shoulder and agree with them -- affirm their deeply held conviction, and start the Feel, Felt, Found procedure. "I agree with you 100%. In fact, I hear that very same thing from many of my customers. They find most foams sleep hot and have horrible off-gassing smells. However, when they experience our foam, they find a very different experience. They find it's supportive, breathable and has none of that horrible scent. Let me show you an example."

Now this is a much more effective way to handle a challenge. You not only maintain control and maintain rapport, you validate their concerns and give them permission to change their mind.

Don't let them off the hook

There is an old saying in negotiating: "He who talks first, loses." Basically, once you ask for a sale, you are supposed to shut up and let the customer feel the pressure to make a decision. In a traditional sales process, it is effective if you are trying to close a sale. The process works off of pressure. With pressure comes discomfort, and if you are the source of discomfort, you are not a friend.

The Objectionless Close process is based on a leading the customer to the solution and removing all concerns. The customer is left with the logical choice and an emotional feeling of satisfaction and relief.

In our stores, we use two techniques to keep the decision-making process focused on making a decision: Choice and Proximity.

Choice

When executing the greeting, we ask questions of the customer to discern their preferences, then inform the customer we are going to lead them to a couple of options. This is important for a couple of reasons. First of all, no one likes to be forced into an option. People like choices. However, too many choices can be counterproductive. On a car lot or in a mattress store, if the customer sees too many options, they can easily get overwhelmed. At a furniture store, if there are 200 sofas and you don't lead the customer to a few that will fulfill their wants and needs, they are going to see 200 sofas and feel overwhelmed.

A well-trained salesperson discovers the customer's wants and needs -- their urgency and desire -- and recommends a few to choose from, helping the customer focus on a few instead of 200. For instance, most mattress stores have 50 to 100 mattresses displaying, and instead of seeing lots of choices, the customer sees a sea of mistakes. They are overwhelmed and get the feeling there is no way they could choose one from so many options. A well-trained salesperson helps them narrow their focus by leading.

By narrowing the choices to two or three, the customer subconsciously begins to decide on one or the other, instead of whether they want to buy from you or another store. This is a key part of making an Objectionless Close, as the customer will likely decide based on your suggestions.

Proximity

By engaging the customer, building intimacy and making friends, the customer will stay longer and be more comfortable in your store. As a friend and trusted advisor, they will welcome you in as a part of the decision making process. From time to time the customer will need some time with their partner or companion or on their own to make the decision.

This is where some salespeople lose the sale by removing themselves from the equation. The worst thing you can do at this juncture of the sales process is get focused on the computer or a menial task away from the sale somewhere else in the store. For one, you cannot observe the customer's body language and you likely will miss the clues that the customer wants you to re-engage or is ready to purchase. Also, the customer may not want to bother you, feeling they may be being rude and interrupting you from whatever other task you are involved with. I have seen customers walk out the door at this point of the sale because the salesperson had -- suddenly and at the most crucial time -- disengaged from them.

Proximity is similar to the "Last one to talk" technique, without the direct pressure. If your customer needs some space or time, you can give them the space they need without removing yourself completely from the equation. Simply find a menial task nearby but out of earshot of the customer, and keep them within your peripheral vision so as not to make the customer feel like they are being watched. Keep an eye out for clues the customer is ready for you to re-engage.

The Counter Is for Love

Yet another important aspect of rapport and maintaining a successful retail relationship is to remember that the sales counter, the cash register and the sales office are for love, not for sales.

You just spent a considerable amount of time and effort creating a safe, warm, trusting environment for your customer, and they rewarded your efforts by making a decision to buy your product or service. The last thing you want to do is to throw a wet blanket on the whole thing by putting pressure on the customer at the counter.

We have all experienced it: You get to the counter, excited to enjoy your purchase, only to have someone try to add on or sell a warranty or some other thing we don't want. It quickly takes away all the fun of the sale and brings pressure and doubt back into the process.

In our mattress stores, we offer a service which provides 10 years of stain removal and accidental damage repair. It's an extended service contract. Two of the worst phone calls I get in this business that I cannot solve are about someone spilling something and how to get out the smell and stain, or about the comfort of the mattress six months after it was purchased. This product solves those issues and is really a great solution if the customer has these concerns. But this must be determined prior to coming to the counter to finalize the purchase. If we were to wait until after the customer comes to the counter, excited about their purchase, only to introduce another product -- no matter how great -- it would make the relationship feel awkward and contrived.

Instead, during the course of the sales conversation, we ask questions about our customer's lifestyle, such as if they sleep with pets or young children. Or, if they have concerns or fears that the mattress would not be comfortable several months down the road, we assure them we have a great service available, which is very affordable, and it will solve their concern if it occurs. By introducing the service and alleviating the fear and concern, the customer effectively just bought the service. All that is left at the end of the sale is an affirmation that they want the service. It is common for the customer to tell our staff they also want to get the service we spoke of during the sale. It is a much more respectful way to introduce the service and leads to the customer choosing it, not us pushing it. Basically, once the customer has said yes, don't give them any more opportunities to say no. "Yes" is associated with good feelings and "No" is attached to negative feelings, and we want to keep our Retail Relationships full of good, positive feelings.

Chapter 7 Staying Sharp

Once you have learned about all of these new techniques, you need to implement them. It is never easy to change learned behaviors. It is awkward and feels strange to say things which are not your own words or to hold your hands in a steepling motion when you never have done so. But if you think about it, the first time you do anything it is usually somewhat awkward. The first time I got up on a bike, snowboard and surfboard, I fell repeatedly. As with any new skill or exercise, you need to practice.

Role play is a salesperson's best friend. It gives you a chance to fall off the bike without losing a sale and driving away an actual customer. Our companies and stores work too hard and spend too much money to practice on customers and risk driving them away. Instead, take the time to role play each of these new techniques, either in front of a mirror with yourself or with a co-worker or family member. After practicing many times, the awkwardness will melt away and they will become a part of your normal default sales process.

One of the great advantages to making these words and techniques your default is that when a customer throws you for a loop, or does or says something to throw you off track, it is simple and natural to get back in control of the sale because you have a plan; you have a new default of what you want to say and do. I have a philosophy in hiring which is, "I would rather hire nice people and teach them to sell than hire salespeople and teach them how to be nice." In other words, when boxed into a corner or at a loss of what to do, nice people will default to being nice. Salespeople will try to push or come across as a salesperson.

Practice your greeting with someone and retrain yourself to make the words your own. Hold your hands in a steepling position when you are relaxed so it becomes familiar. Role play taking control of a question with other salespeople on your sales floor, drilling down into it and finishing it with another question. Role playing will make these techniques a part of your toolbox and help you become the most successful salesperson you can possibly become.

Sales Surveys

I created a tool for my sales team called the Sales Survey. Here is an example of the Sales Survey:

Sales Survey
Please fill this out after each customer.

What was your customer's first name(s)? *

How would you rate your overall performance on this sale? 1=Worst 10=Best

What did you do great? *eg. Did they buy? Did you discover an objection before they voiced it?

What could you improve on? *eg. could have used their name more

What was their urgency?

What was their desire? *

Did they buy? *

- yes

- no

The Sales Survey can be customized for your selling environment, but the example shown should give you an idea of what we want to accomplish. Why use a Sales Survey?

When building a house, you use a level to set your foundation; otherwise the entire building will not be level and square, leading the building to be compromised and unstable. Basically, any mistake made at the beginning of the building will be compounded as the building progresses. The same goes for our sales skills. In my experience, the biggest enemy of a salesperson is picking up unproductive aspects in their speech, words, tone or body language subconsciously. Salespeople are like snowballs: the more they roll, the more they accumulate.

The Sales Survey is a tool, not unlike a level, which gives the salesperson reason to pause and self-evaluate their performance after each customer interaction. It helps them identify where they may have deviated from proper techniques, or where they forgot an important aspect of the sales process. It helps bring us back to the "level" level in our minds and helps prevent accumulating things which could negatively affect the outcome of our sale.

Thank You

As with any relationship, it is a common courtesy to say "Thank You" to a customer for purchasing from us. It is a classy move to take the time at the end of your day and write out a handwritten thank-you card to a customer with whom we have just built a great Retail Relationship. Very few companies do this anymore, electing to send out email blasts or junk mail instead. A handwritten card is a powerful rapport-builder after the sale and maintains the great and profitable Retail Relationship you just built with your customer.

In our store in Hawai'i, our company was smart enough to incentivize this process by tying the writing of thank-you cards to the sales staff's monthly bonus. Not all salespeople will be motivated to write a thank-you card, but everyone likes money. The relationship developed in the store is a valuable one, and customers love to tell their friends on social networks about a new purchase and experience, which leads to more customers and more sales. A thank-you card -- a nicely handwritten note -- ensures that your customer knows that they are very important to you and your company. It's the right thing to do in maintaining a profitable and enjoyable Retail Relationship with a valued customer.

Does this stuff work?

I have always been among the top performers in any company I have worked for in a sales capacity. And when asked by the other salespeople how I did it, I would gladly share my techniques. But never have I shared them to this extent or this thoroughly.

I believe this is the most powerful way to sell you will ever learn. I tell my salespeople who train and work with me that wherever they go to sell, they will always be one of the top producers because of this training.

You can call any of my past employers and they will affirm my track record. You can go to Yelp.com in the City of San Francisco and look up the Yelp reviews for the Nest Bedding sales staff I currently manage. We are tops in the city. Customers have glowing things to say about our team. They use their names in the reviews because they remember our staff's names. They like our sales staff because they don't push, they lead.

When I ran a large furniture operation in Northern California, I had seven salespeople to manage in a 55,000-square-foot furniture store. I had a lot of responsibilities, and I also sold. I was routinely the top-producing salesperson, while increasing the stores overall sales to record-setting numbers.

One year I decided to move to Hawai'i and work for a famous family-owned furniture operation. The first year I worked for them I sold 1.75 million dollars in mattresses. In Hawai'i. The nearest salesperson to me was a quarter of a million dollars behind.. They had mattress stores, furniture stores and high-end stores all around the Hawai'ian islands. They employed over 175 salespeople at that time. I was Number One out of all those salespeople for the majority of the year. And I was only selling mattresses. Most of those near the top were selling high-end furniture. There were days when salespeople from the other stores would come asking for this Joe Alexander guy at the top of the list, and then pepper me with questions about how I was doing it.

When I moved back to California a few years later, I worked for one month at an Ashley's Home Furnishings Store in Northern California. They had 10 salespeople and they told me they had never had a new salesperson sell 100K in their first month. I did 199K in sales.

The stores I own now, where we employ my sales training, are very successful and have unheard-of closing rates. We routinely outperform our competitors who have 10 to 20 times the selection we have and mattresses that are two, three and four times the price of ours.

I tell you these things not to brag, but to show you that these techniques work. They have worked for me for years, earning me consistently higher paychecks than my peers, and they have worked in several different settings consistently. I have seen increases in sales for companies I have consulted with and for whom I have worked. And you don't have to have a mattress store for these techniques to work. I recently worked with a veterinarian who, once they applied these techniques, saw their revenue shoot through the roof. If you apply these techniques as a salesperson or to your sales staff, and if you implement these tools into your selling environment, you will see increases in both total sales and in the amount of referral business you get. And at the end of the day, you will feel better about yourself and your job, knowing you are making a difference in the lives of your customers. Making a living and building Retail Relationships.

About the Author

Joseph Alexander has been selling professionally for almost 30 years and has either worked in Sales, Sales Management, Training and Business Ownership during that time. Joseph currently owns 3 successful retail stores called Nest Bedding in Northern California. He is available for personal training sessions and retail sales seminars. Joseph is the proud father of three adult children, is an avid baseball player, singer and surfer.